Learn to Draw Flower Pencil Drawings Step by Step

Pencil Drawing Ideas for Absolute Beginners

By Gala Publication

Published by:

Gala Publication

ISBN-13: 978-1508533733
ISBN-10: 1508533733

©Copyright 2015 – Gala Publication

By Gala Publication

Table Of Content :

How To Draw Gardenia

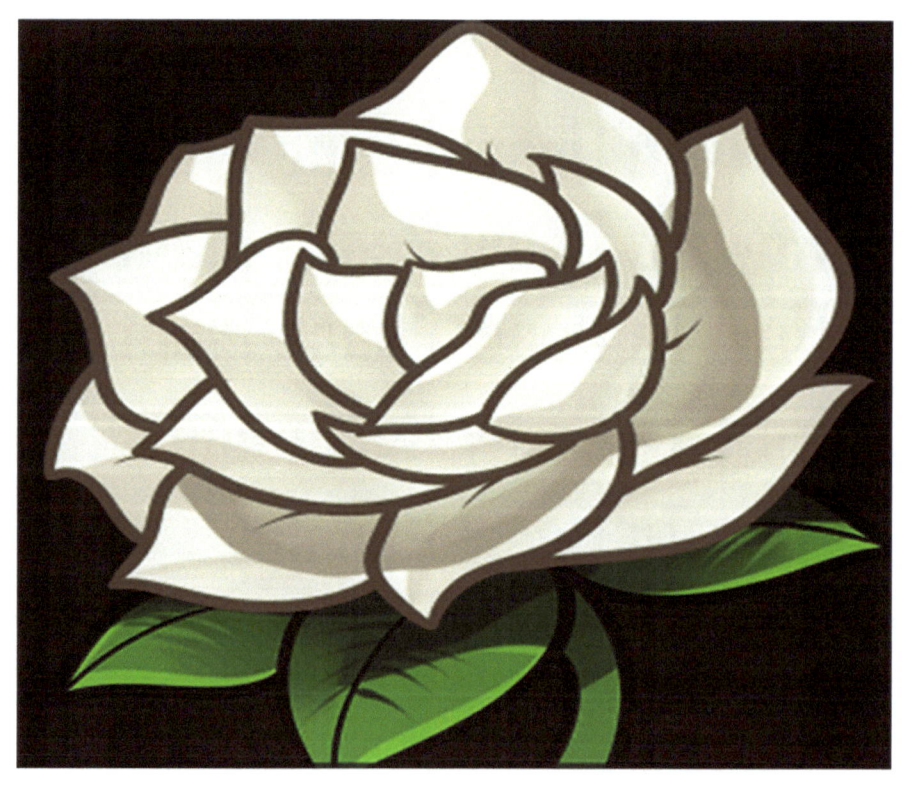

Step 1

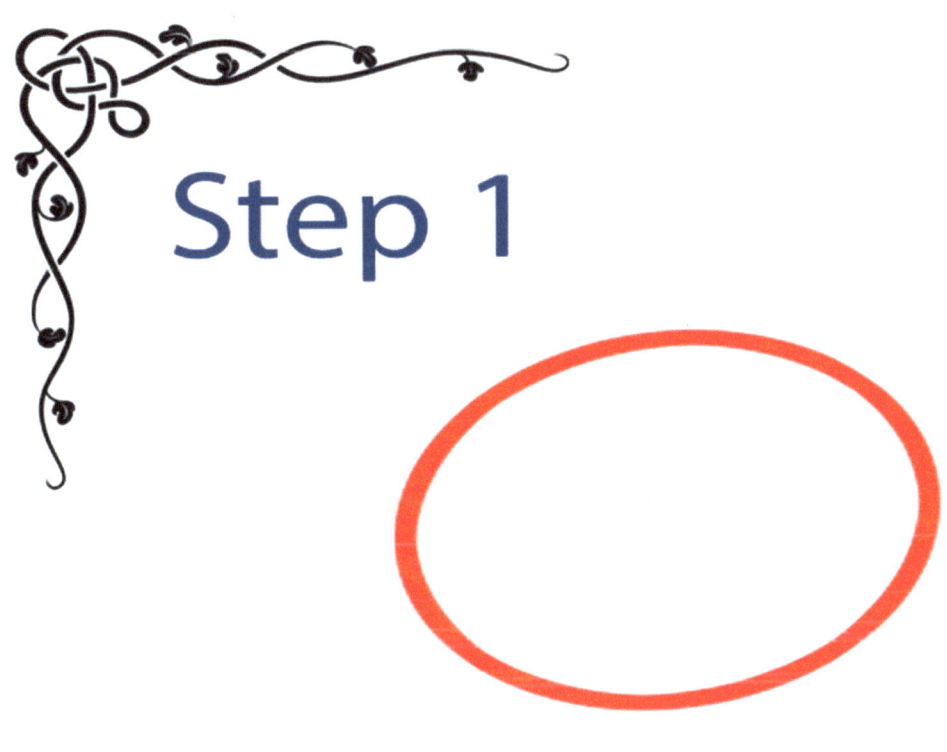

Step 2

Step 3

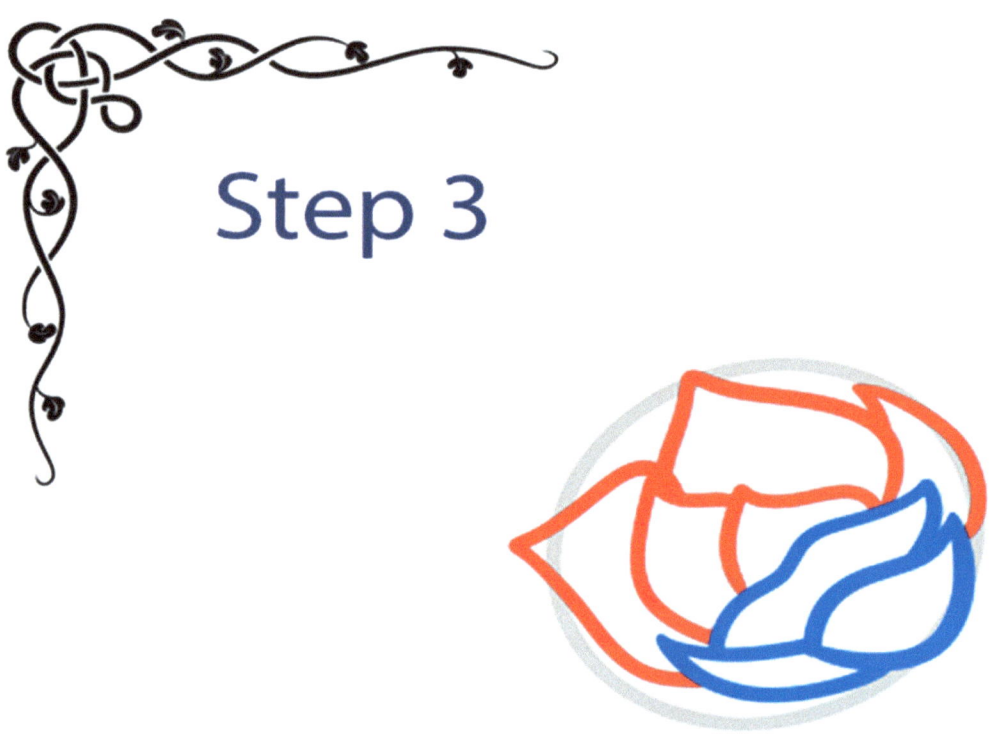

Step 4

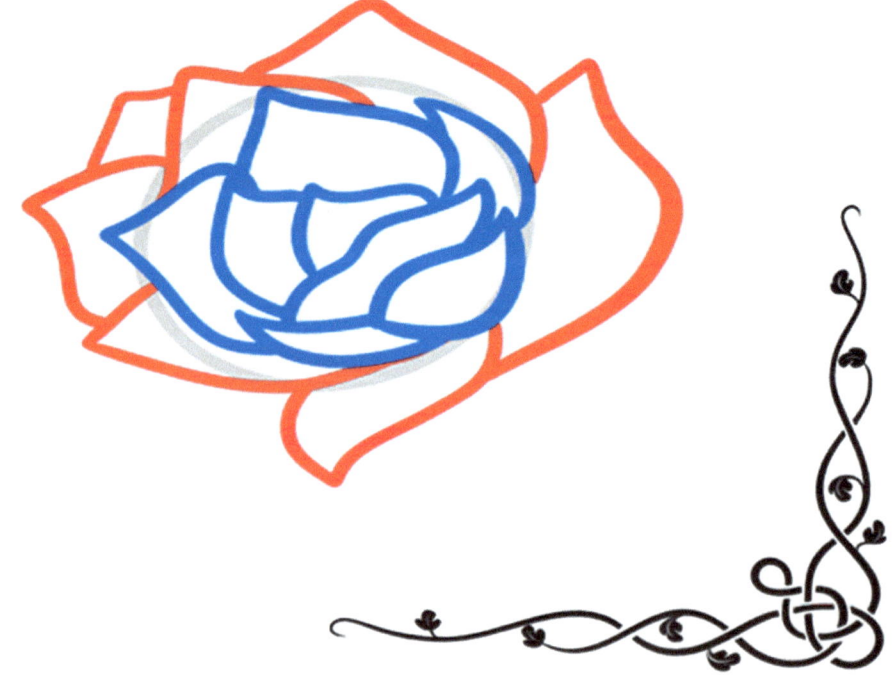

How To Draw a Narcissus

Step 1

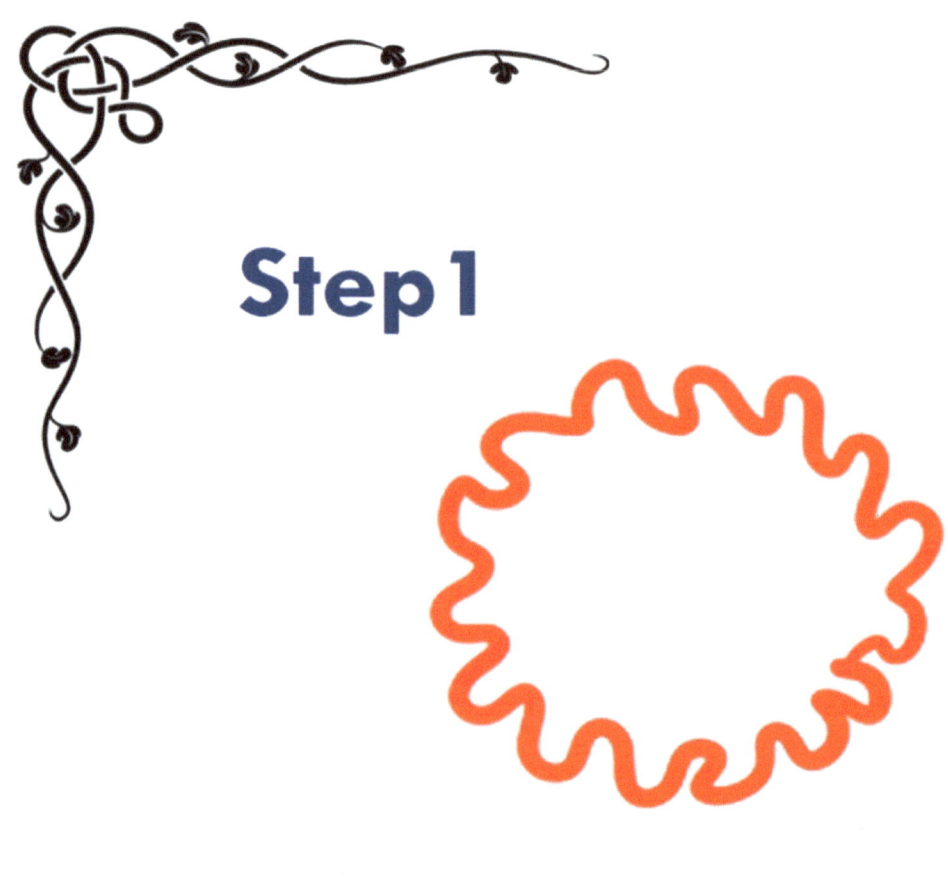

Step 2

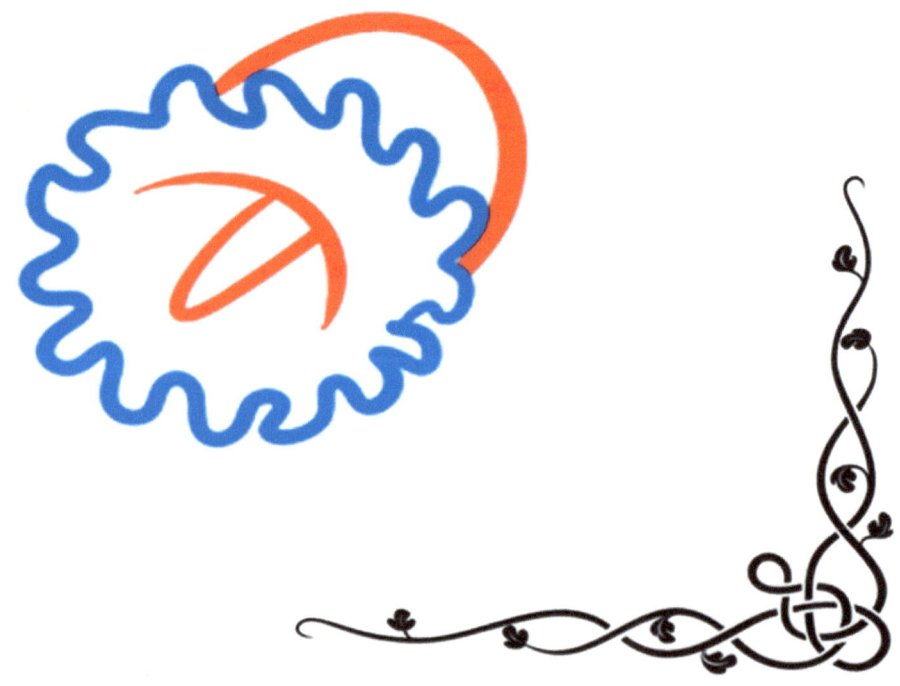

Step3

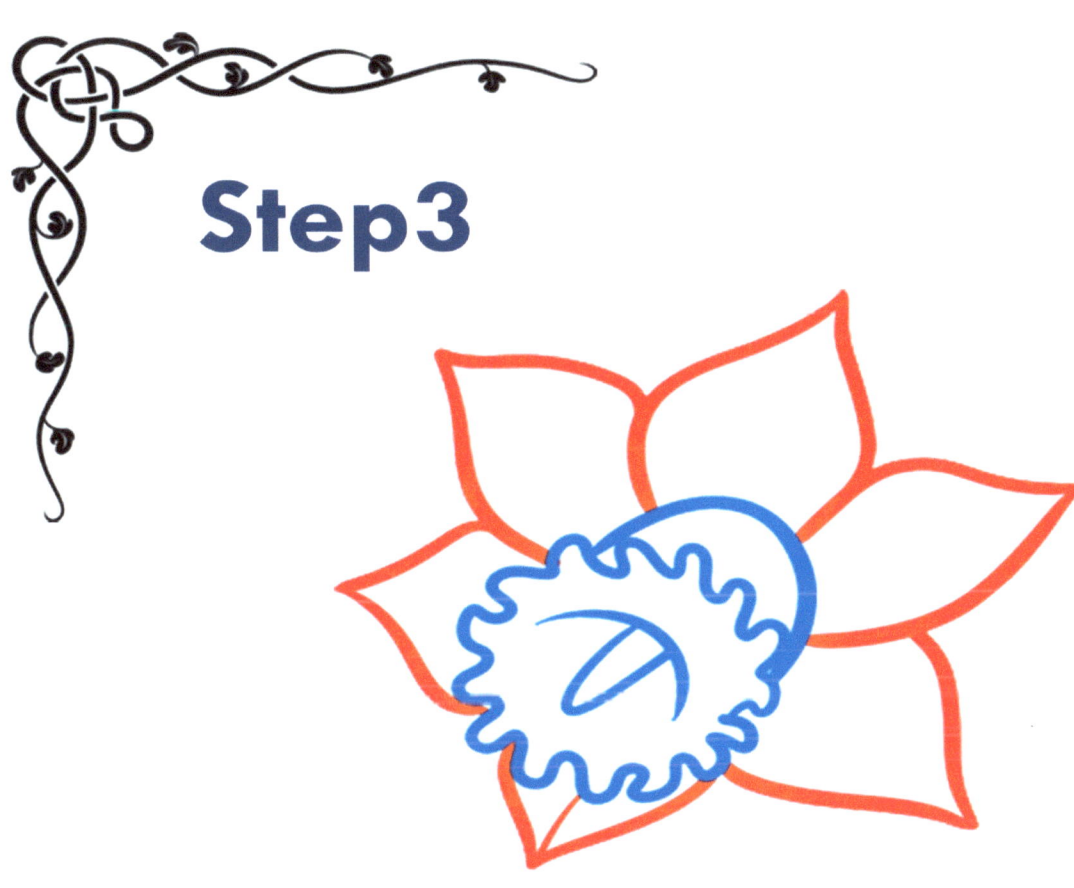

Step 4

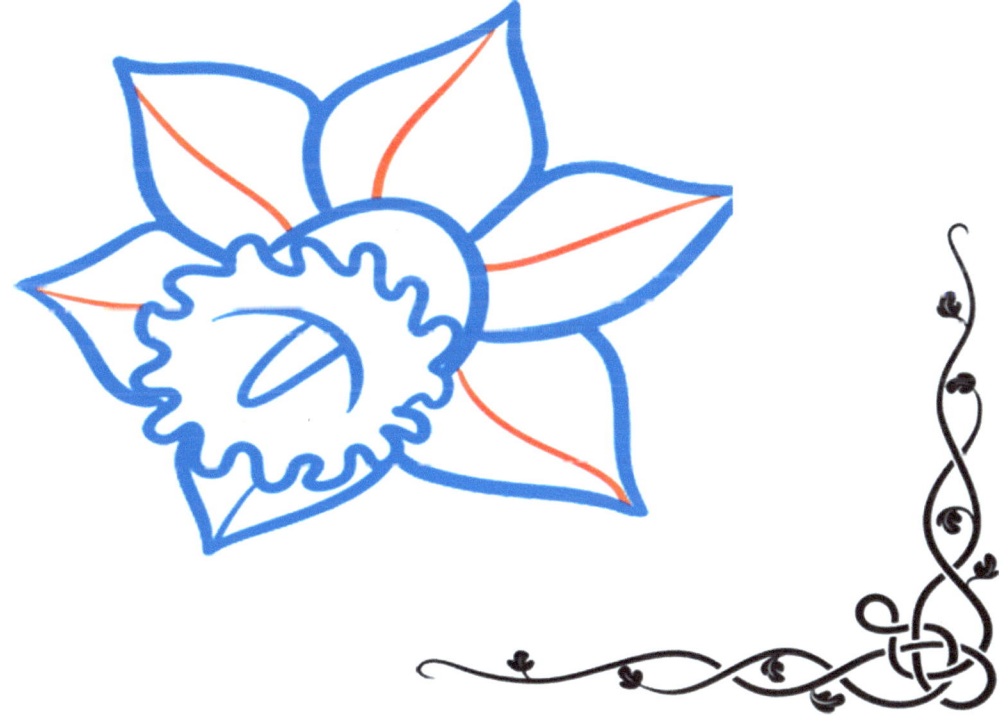

Step 5

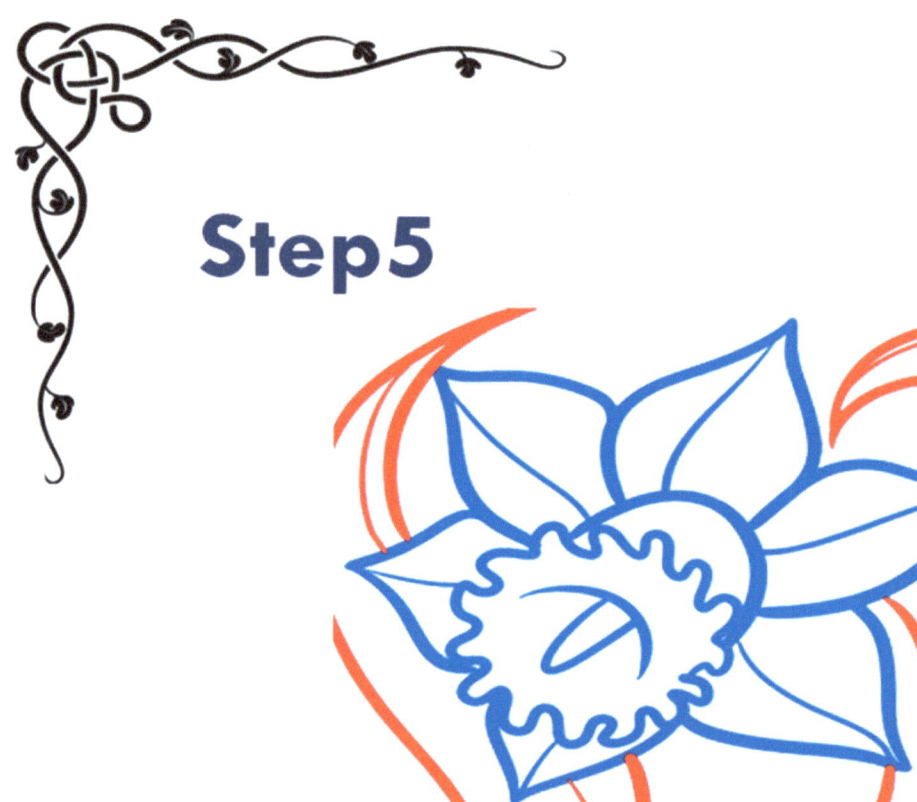

Step 6

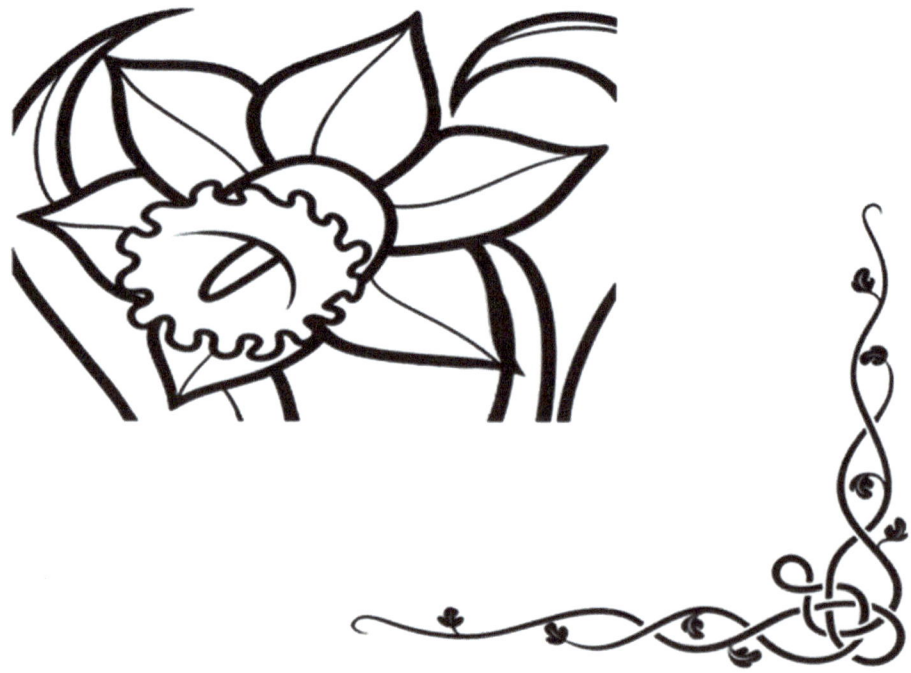

How To Draw
Clover Blossoms

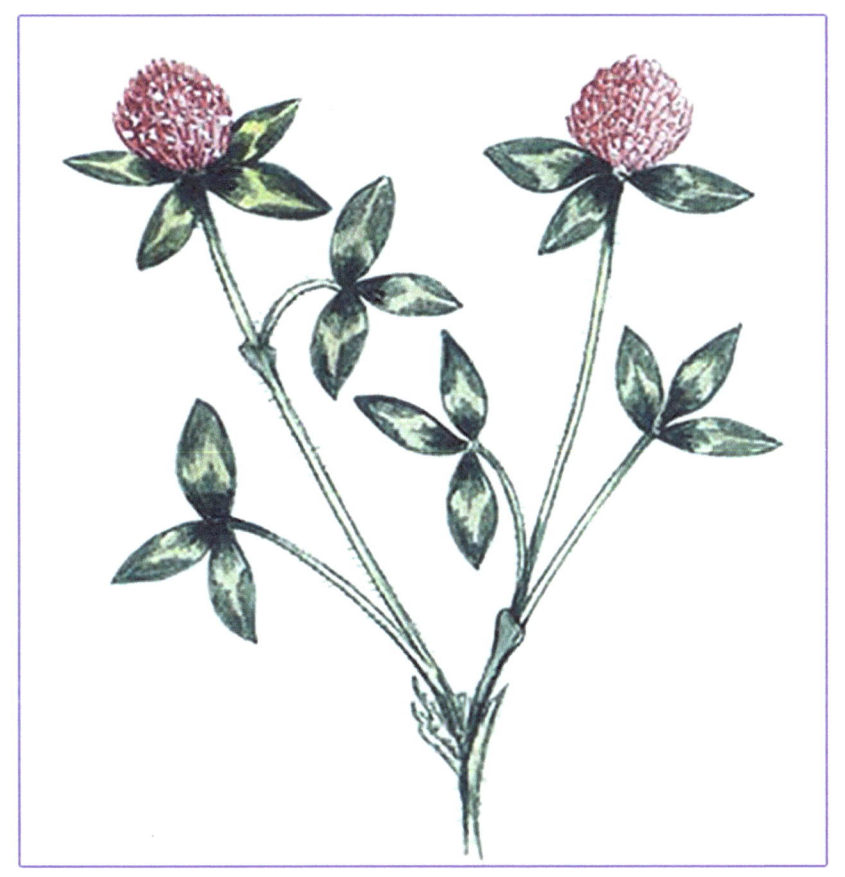

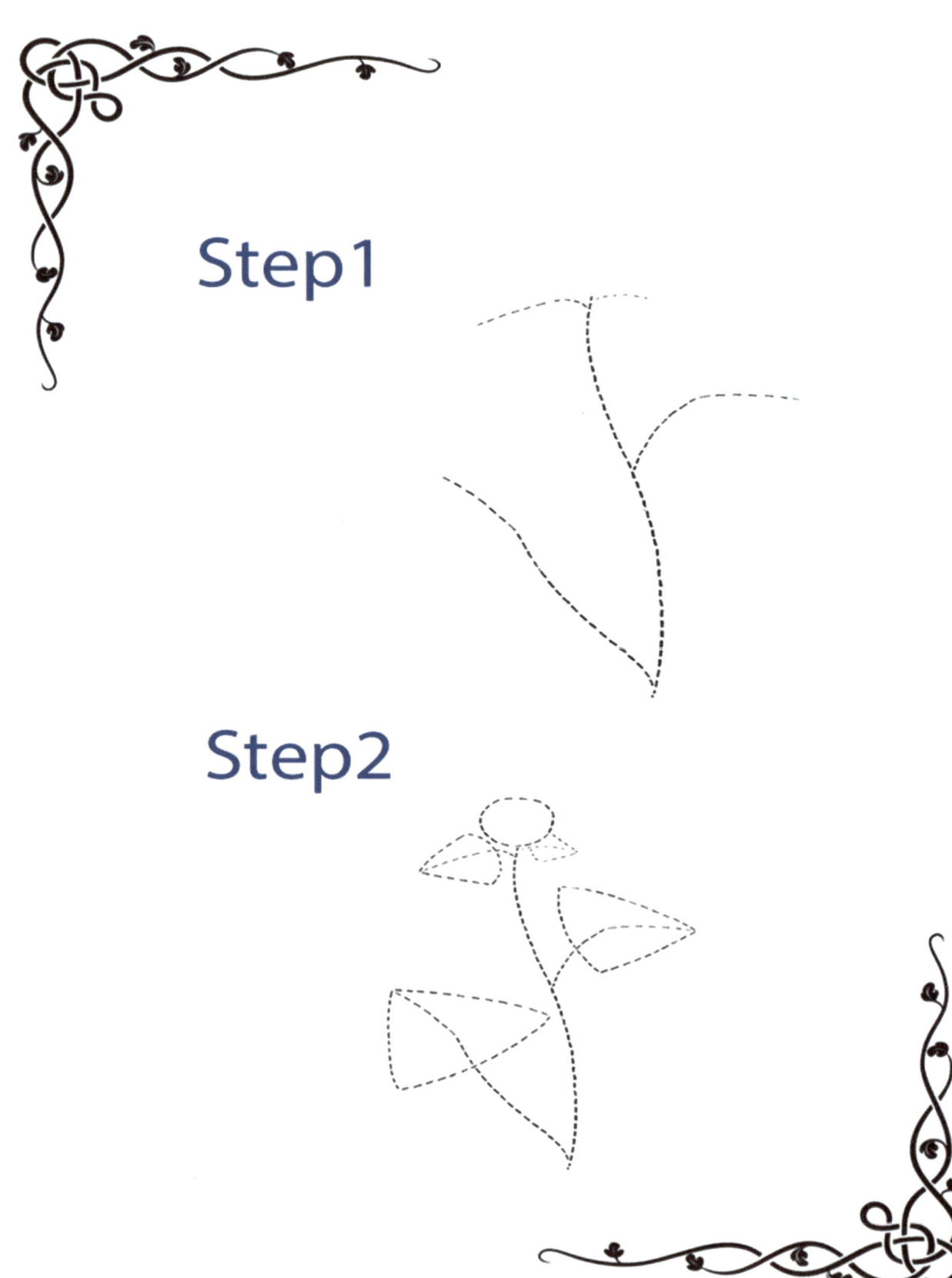

Step1

Step2

Step 3

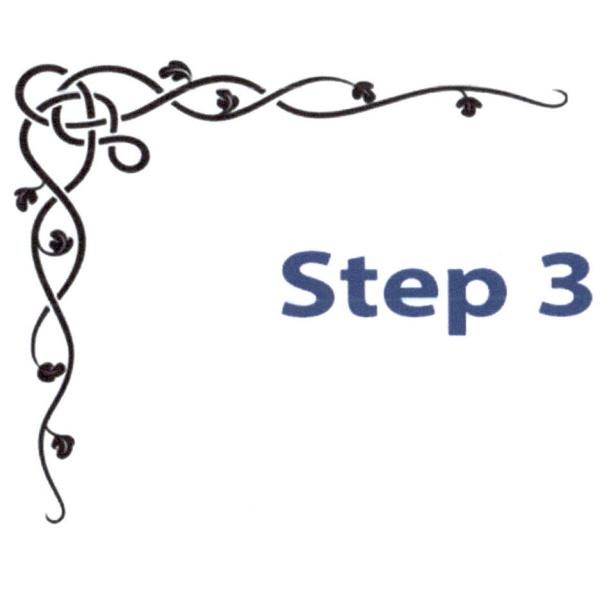

Step 4

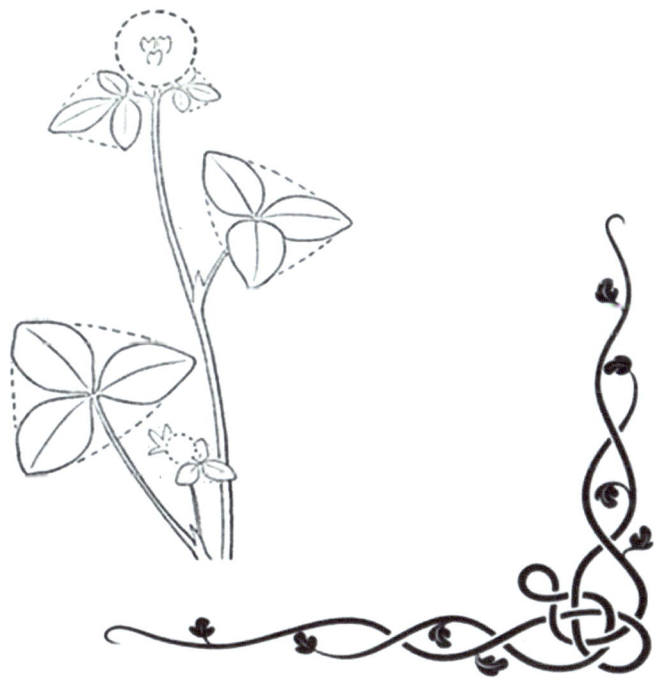

How to Draw
Daffodil

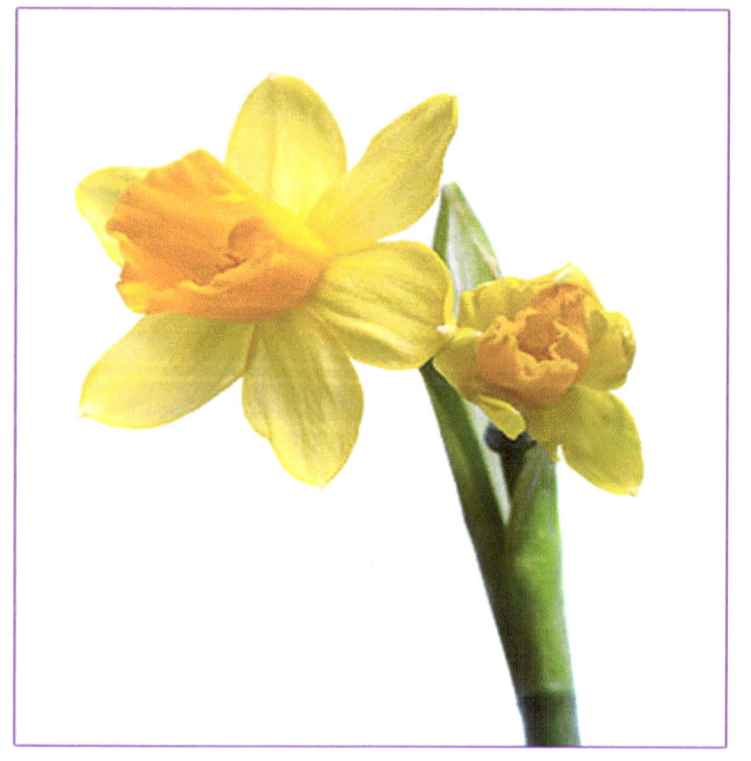

Step 1

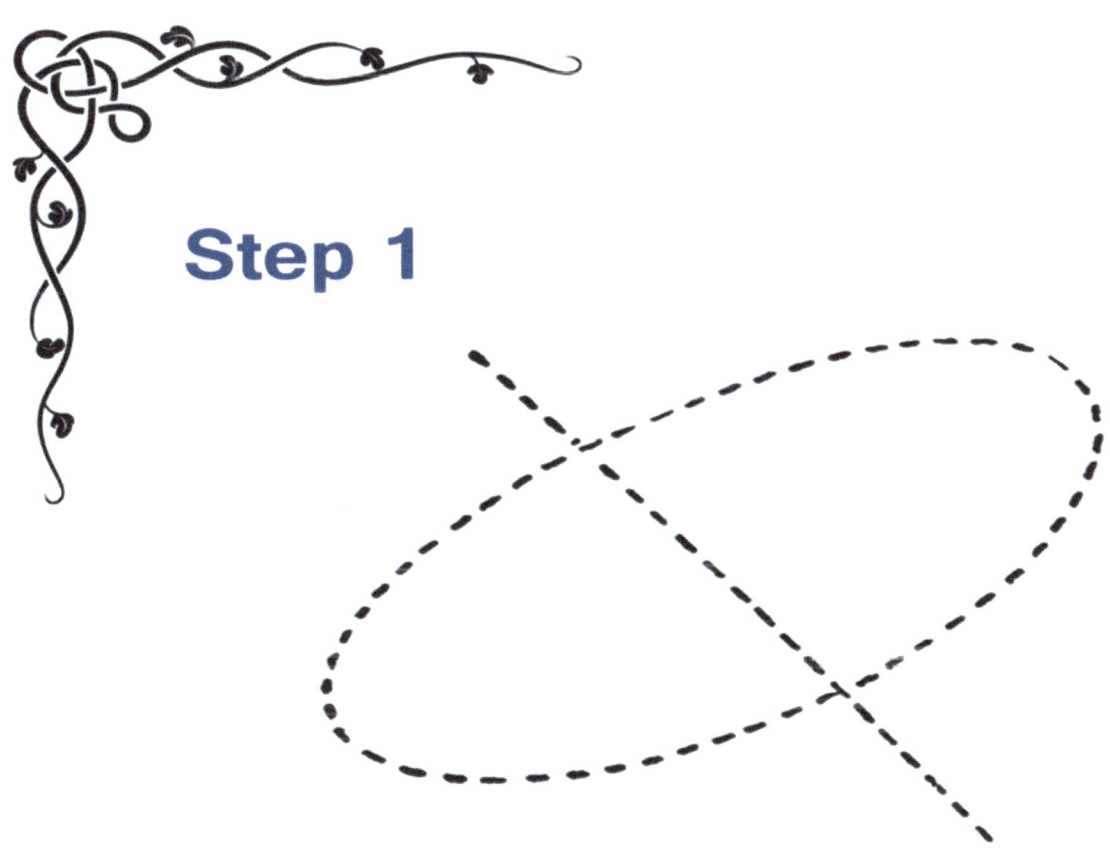

Step 2

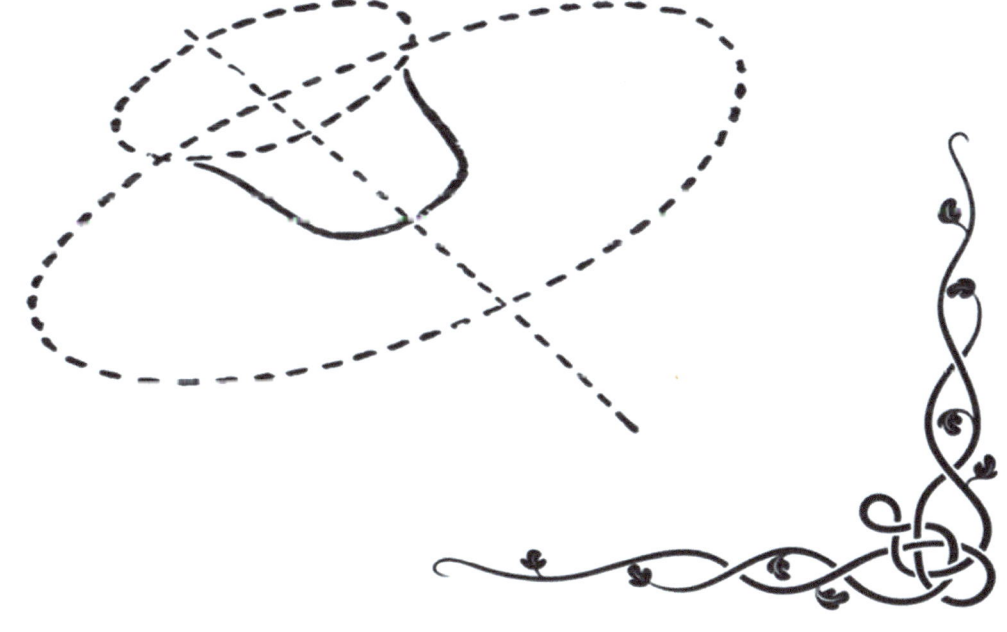

Step 3

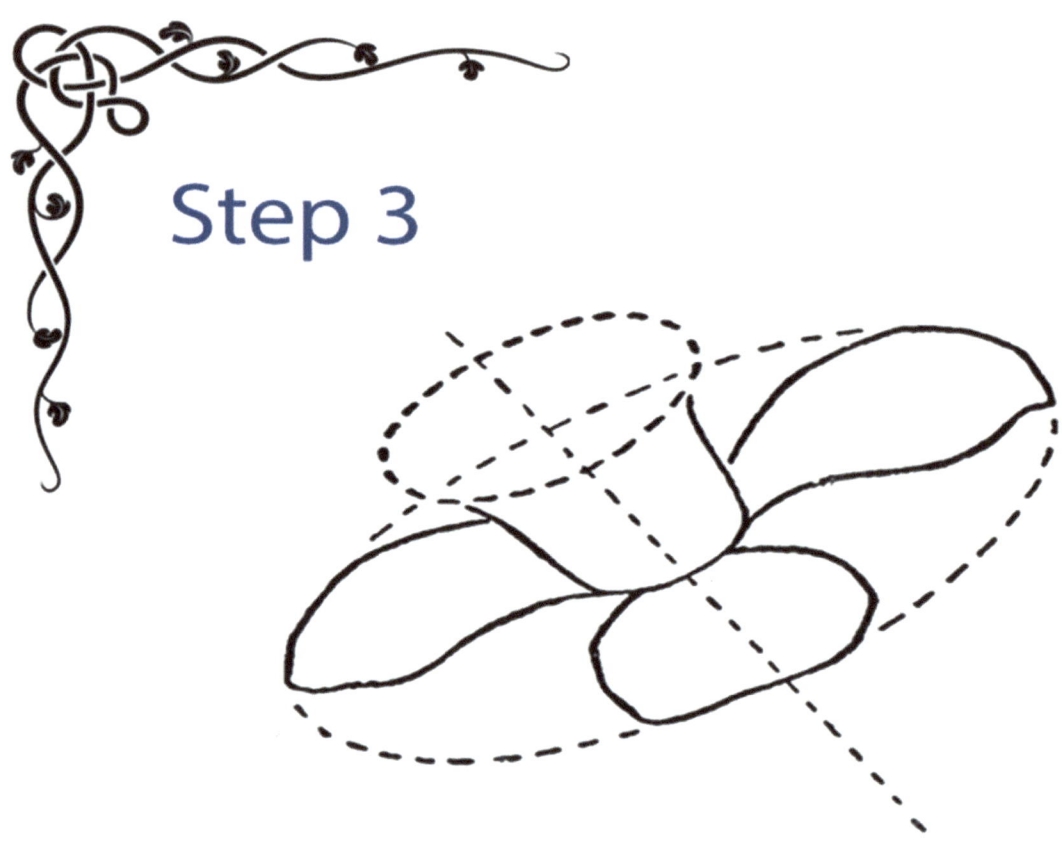

Step 4

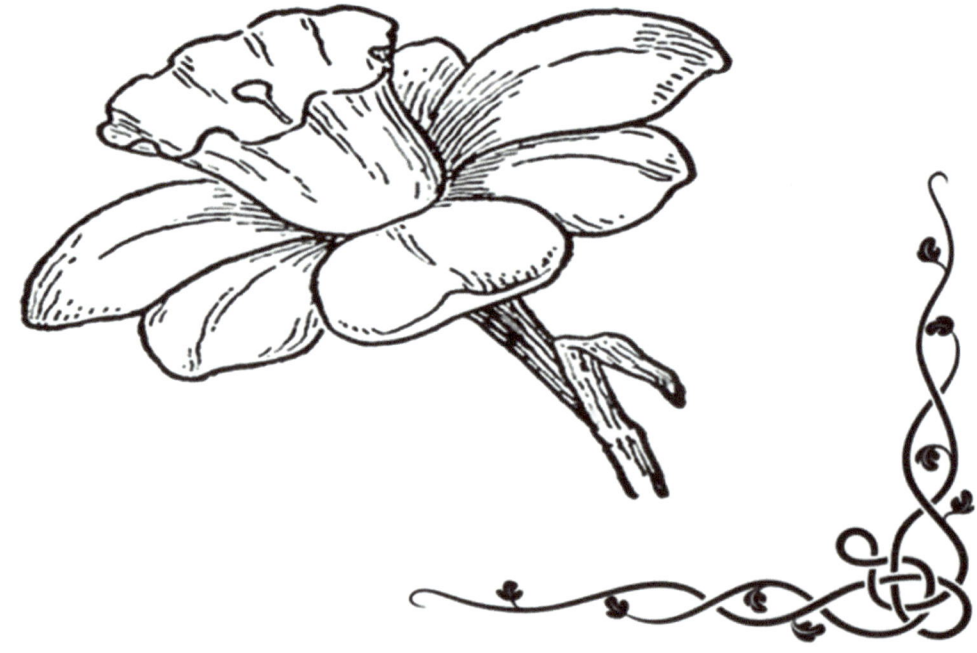

How To Draw
Dahlia

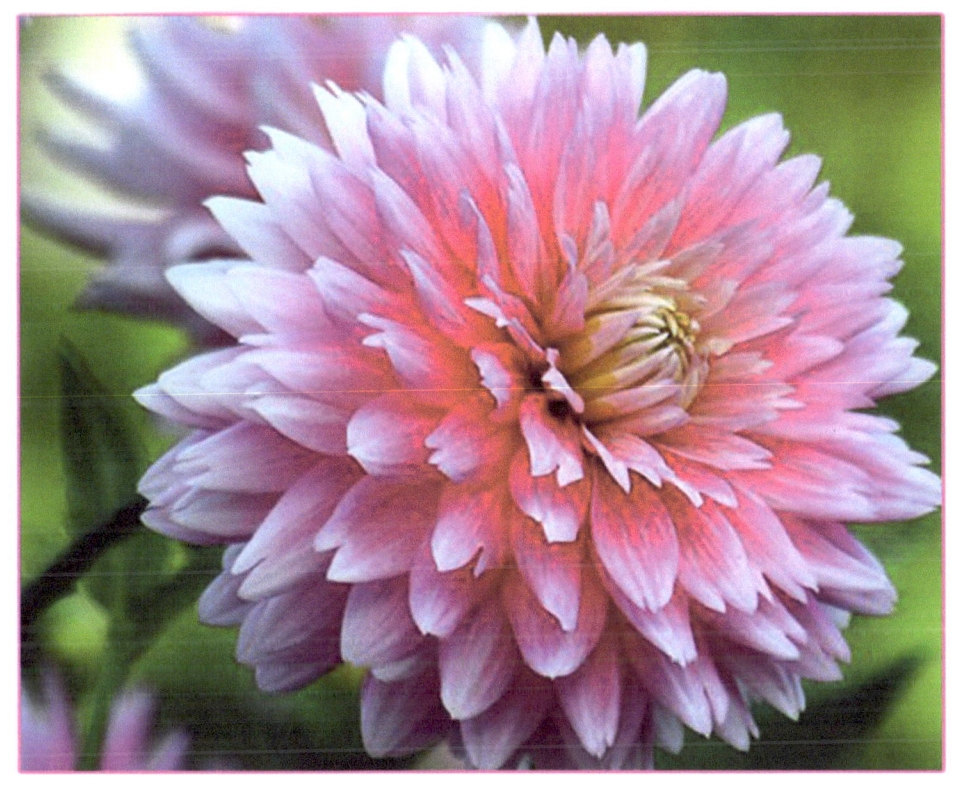

Step 1

Step 2

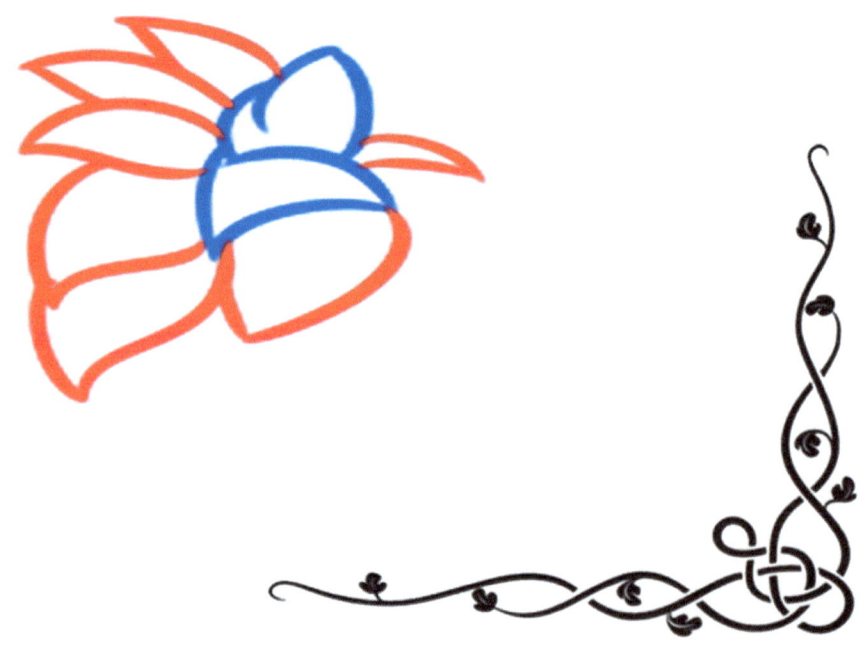

Step 3

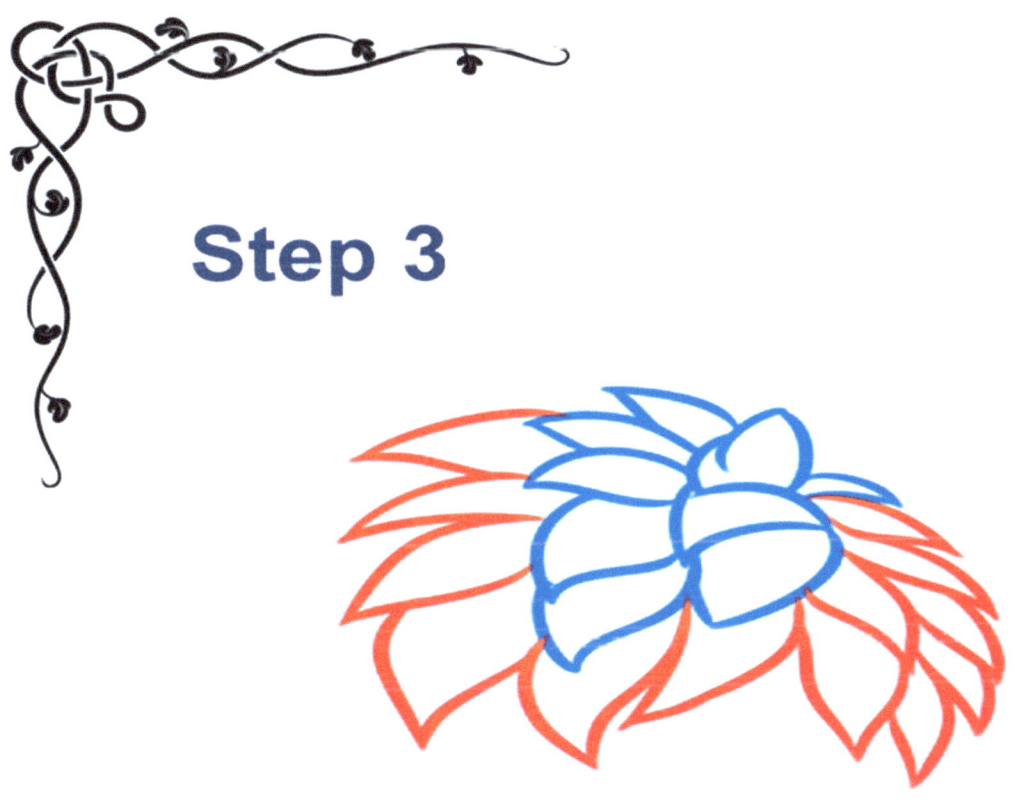

Step 4

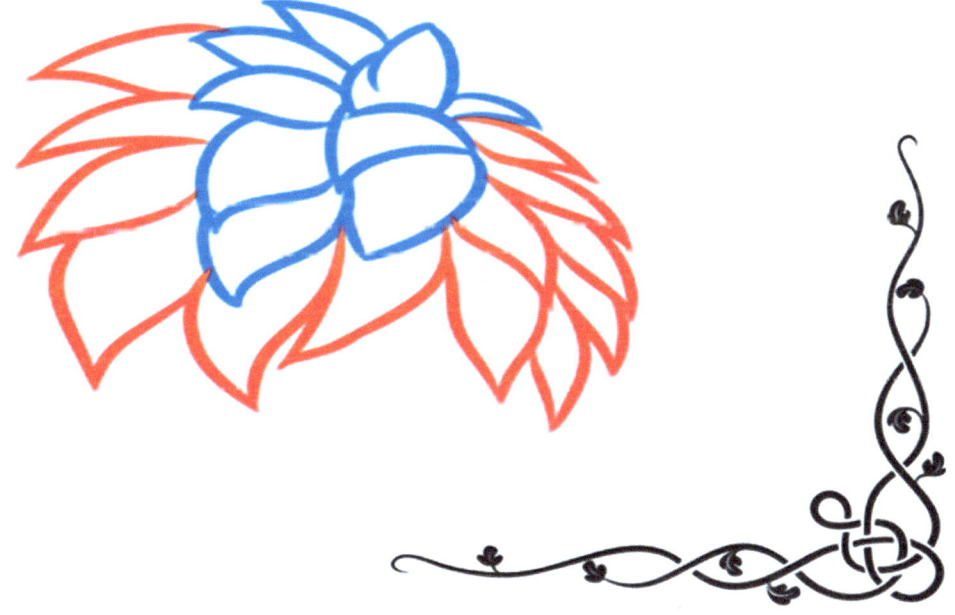

Step 5

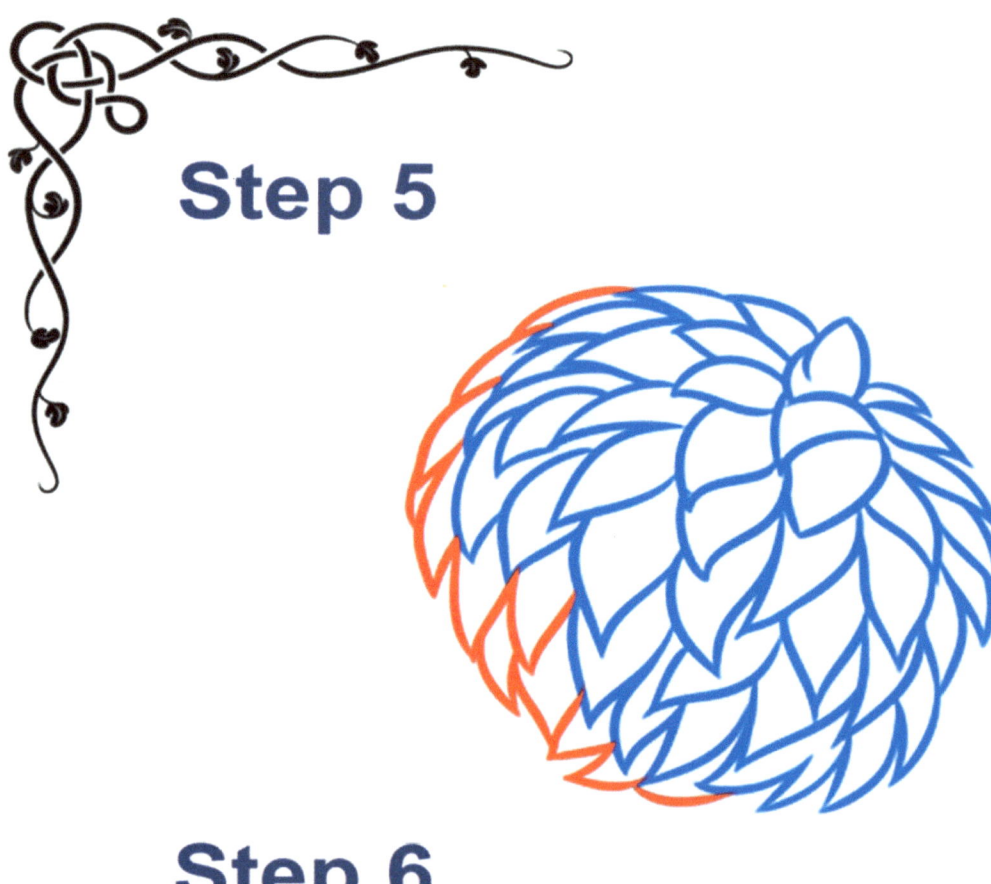

Step 6

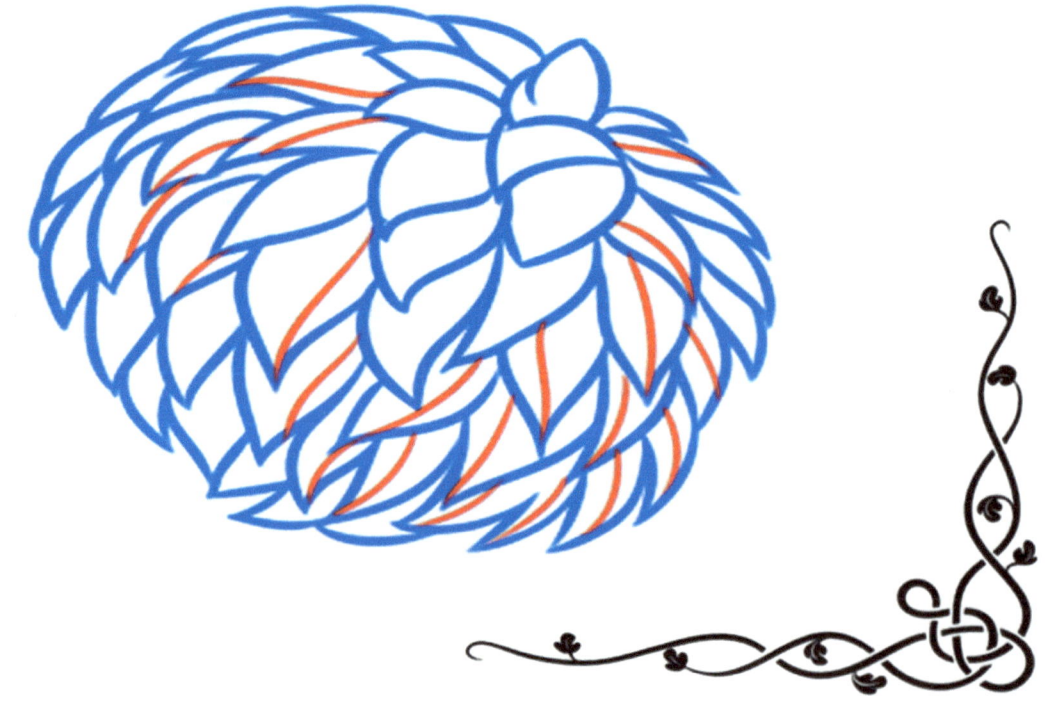

How To Draw
Easter Lily

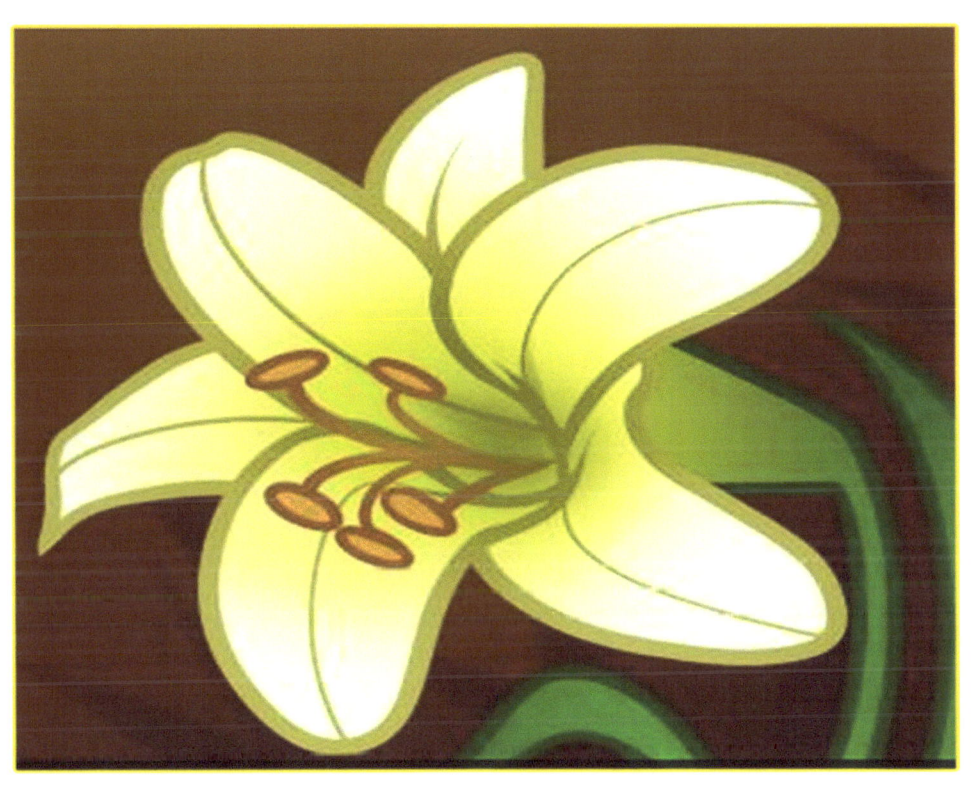

Step 1

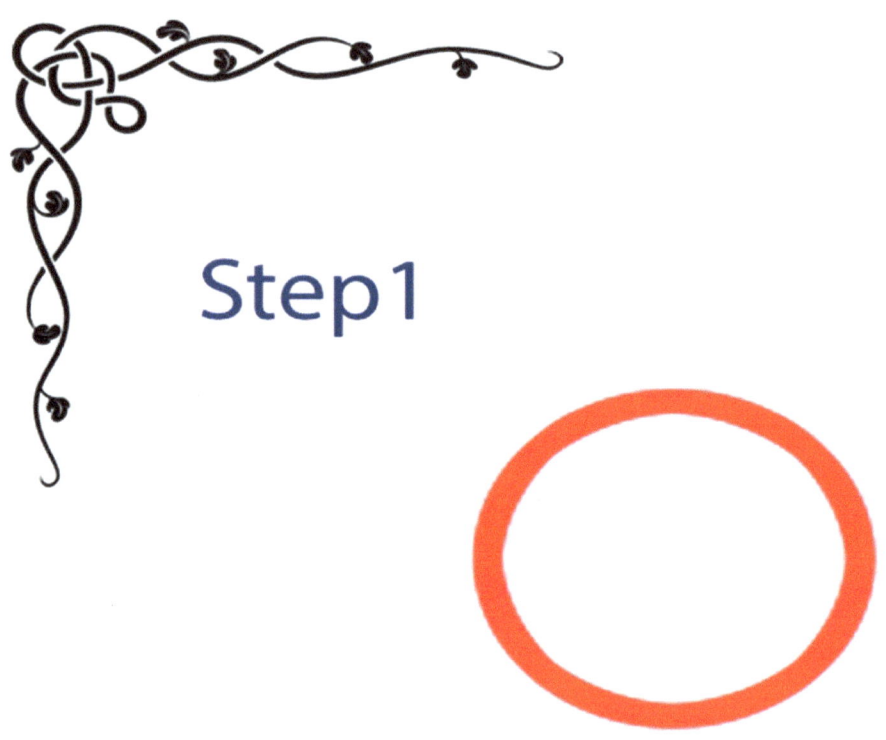

Step 2

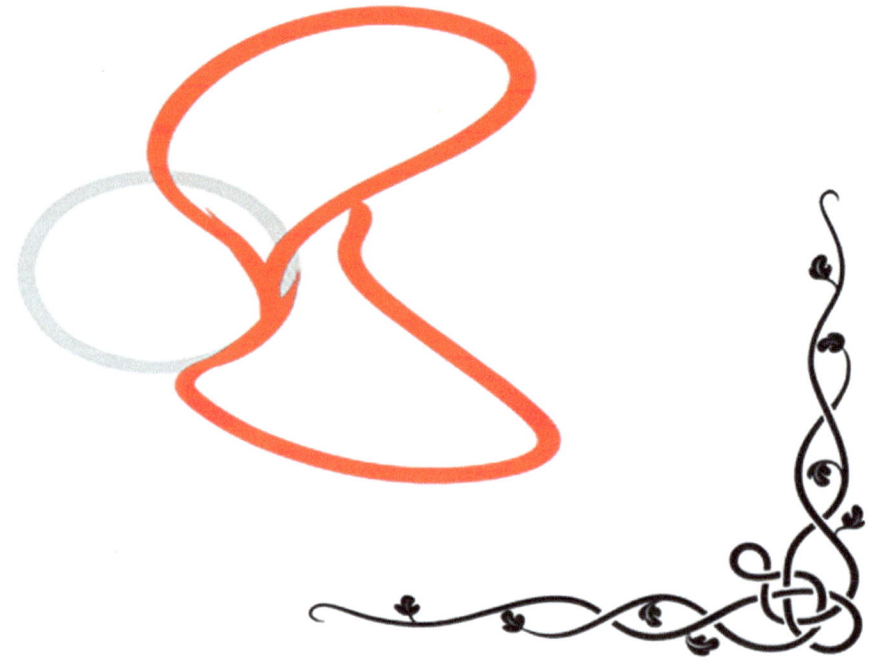

Step 3

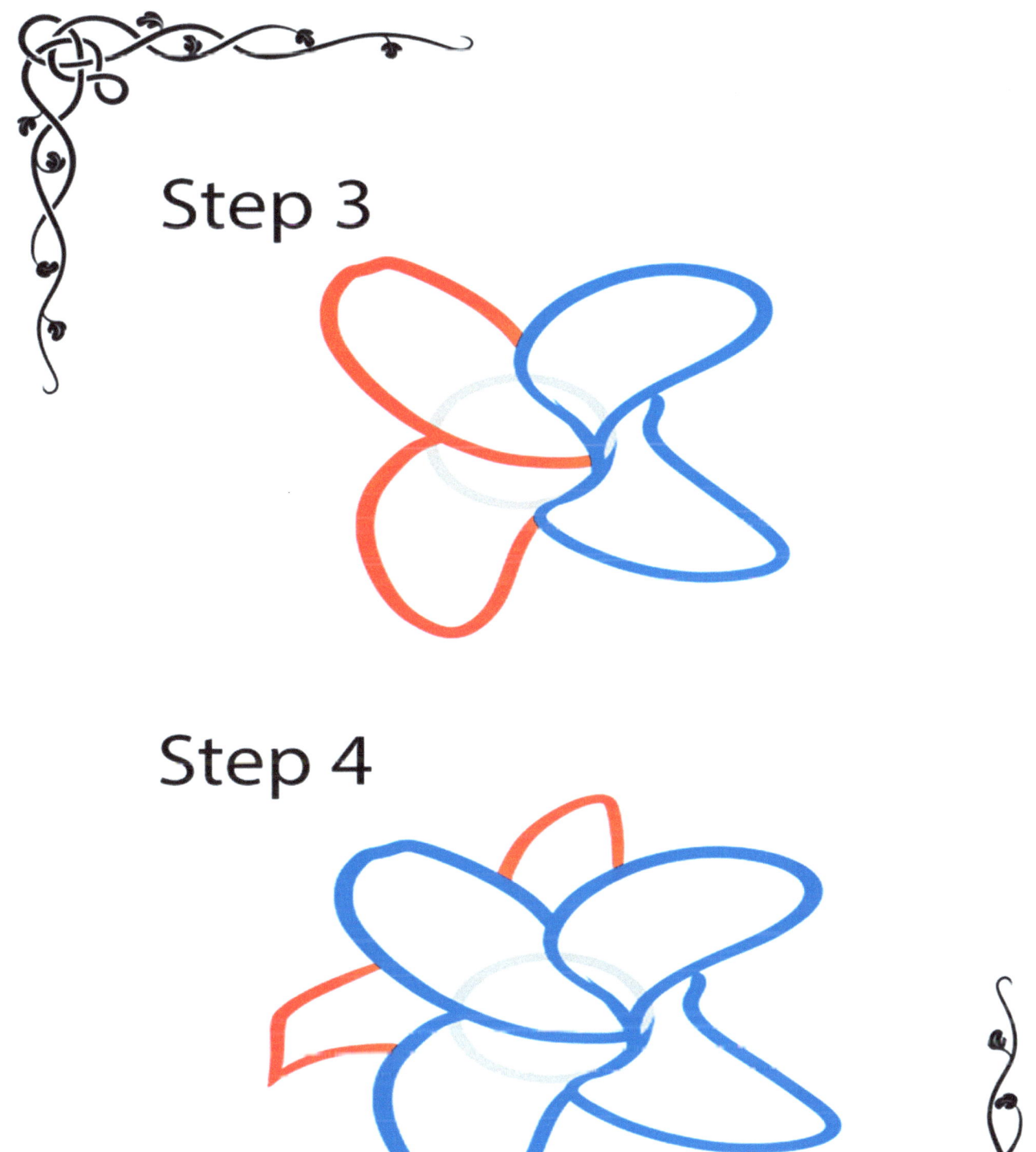

Step 4

Step 5

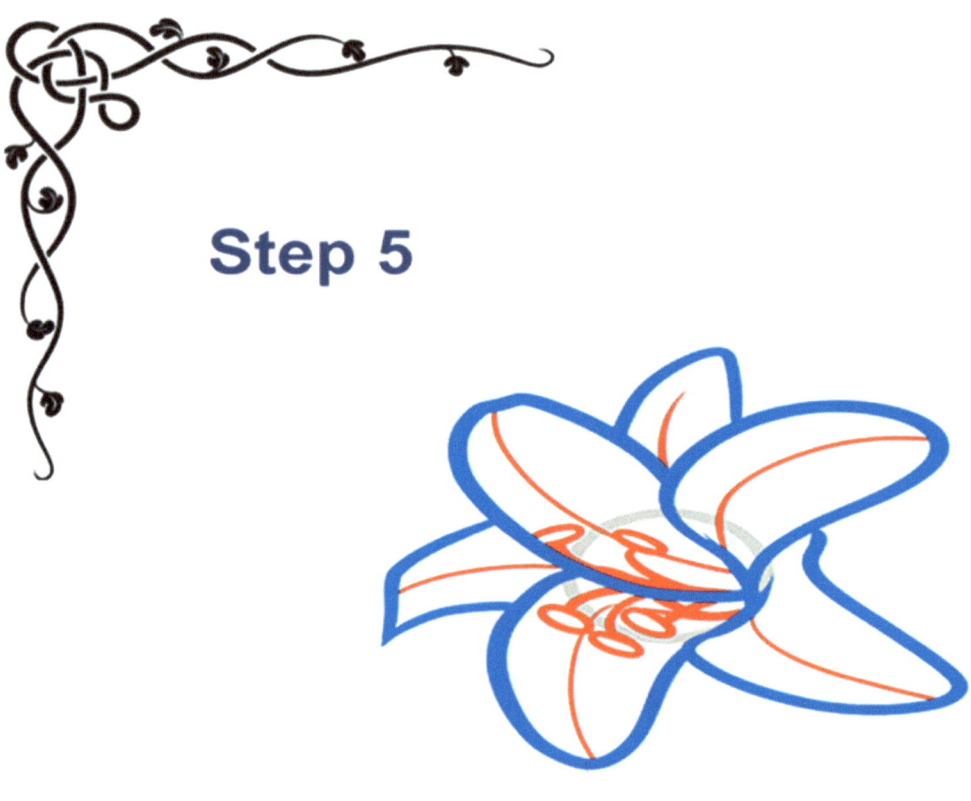

Step 6

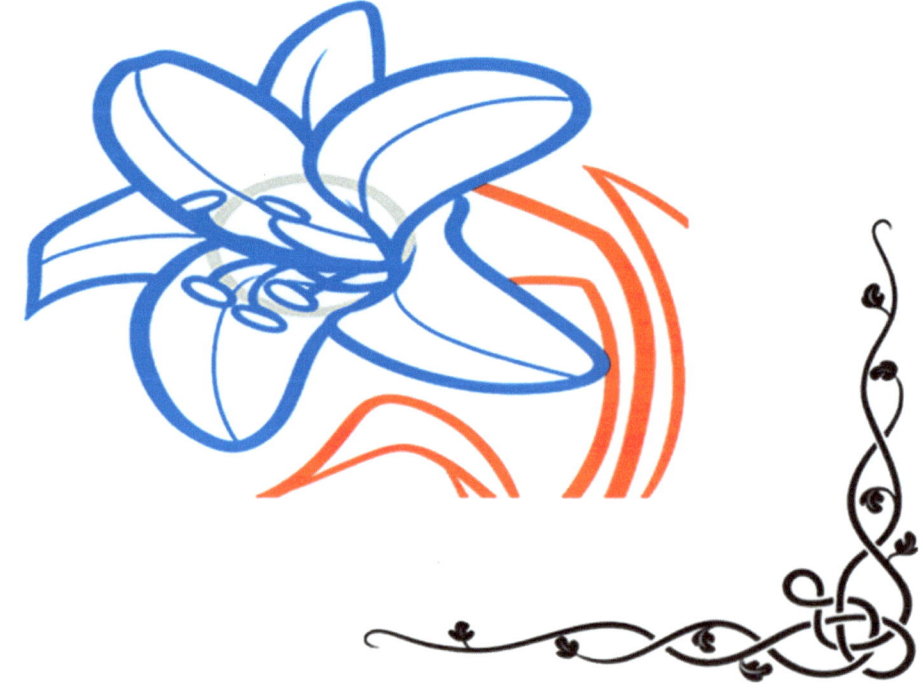

How To Draw
Peace Plant

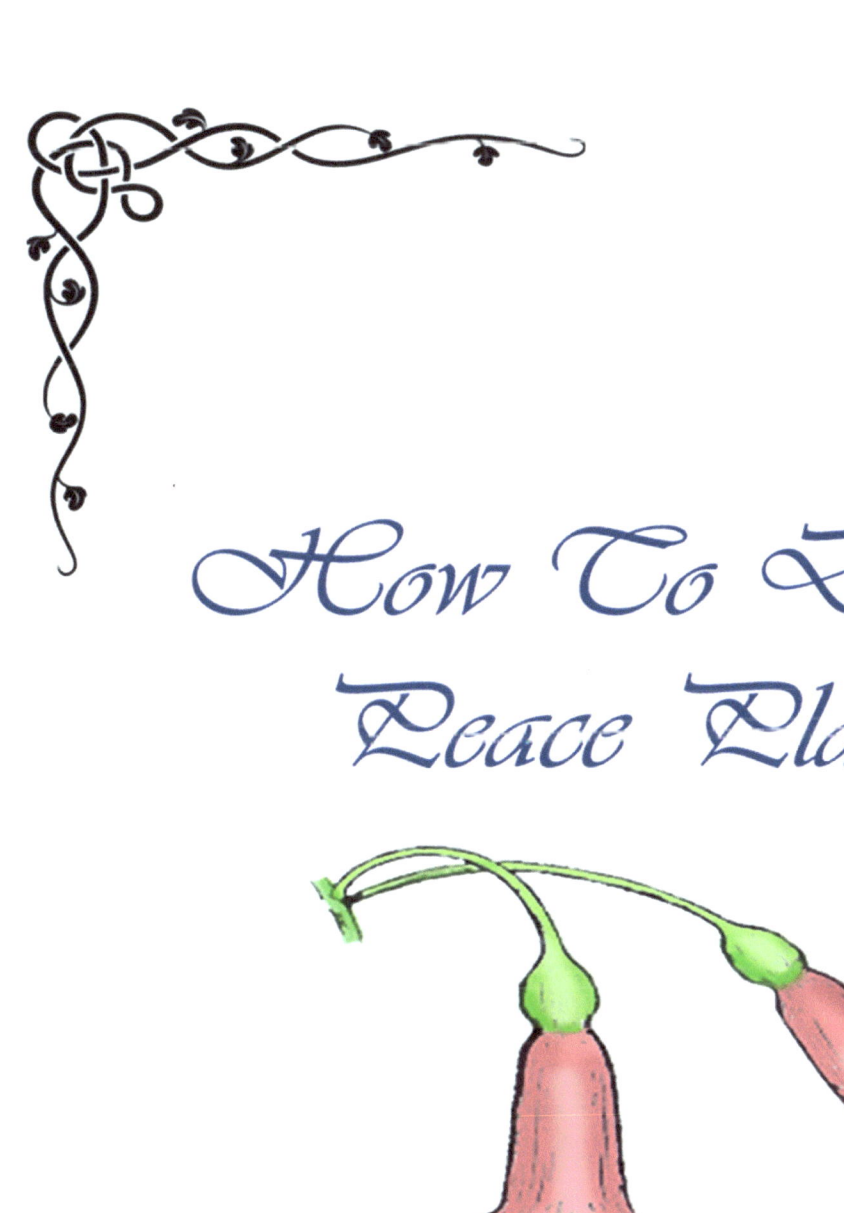

Step 1

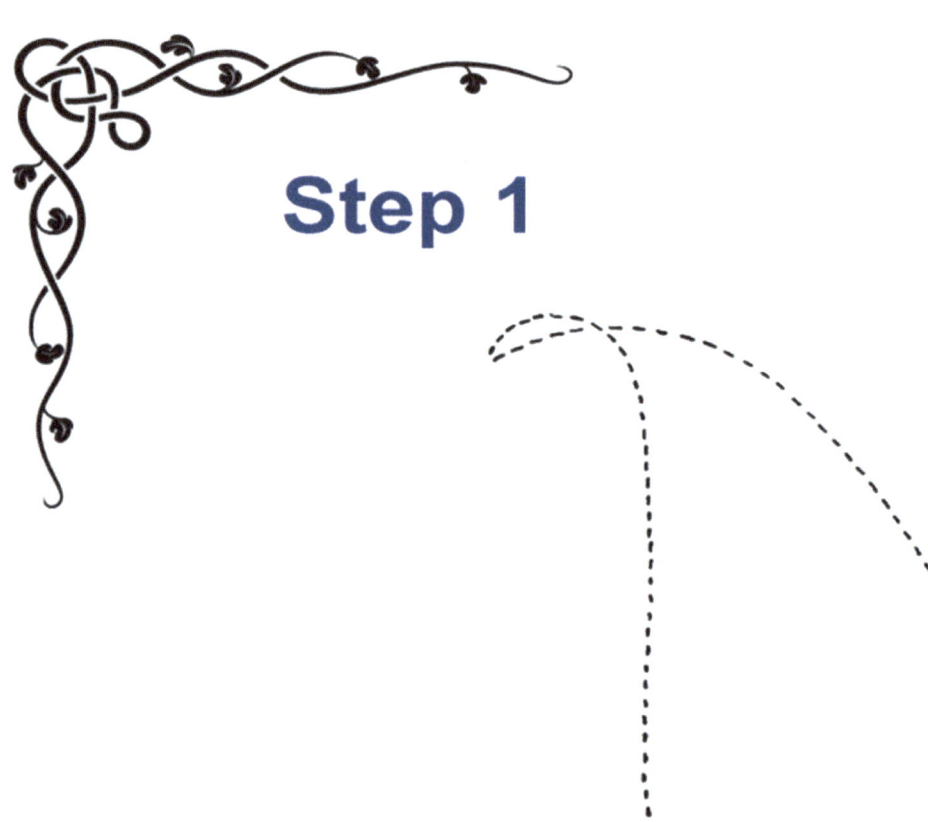

Step 2

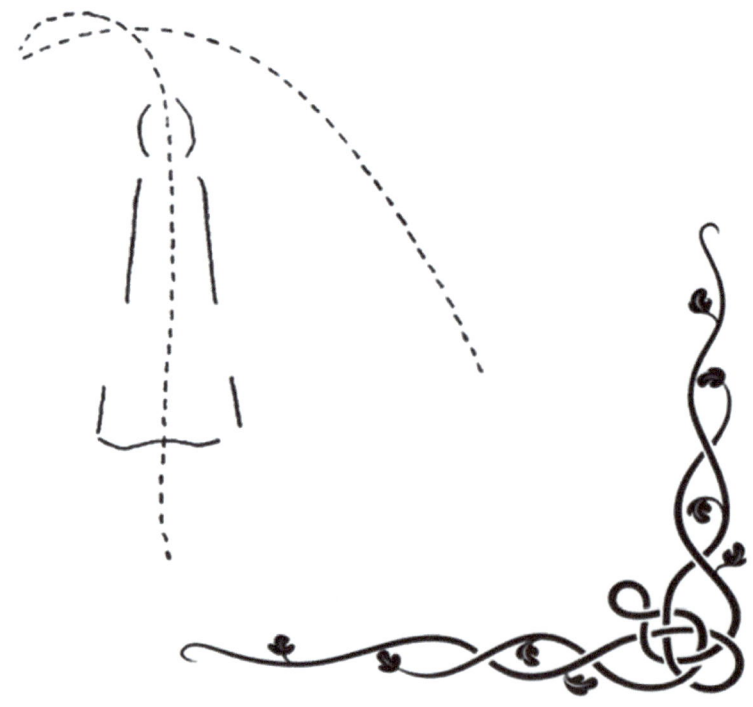

Step 3

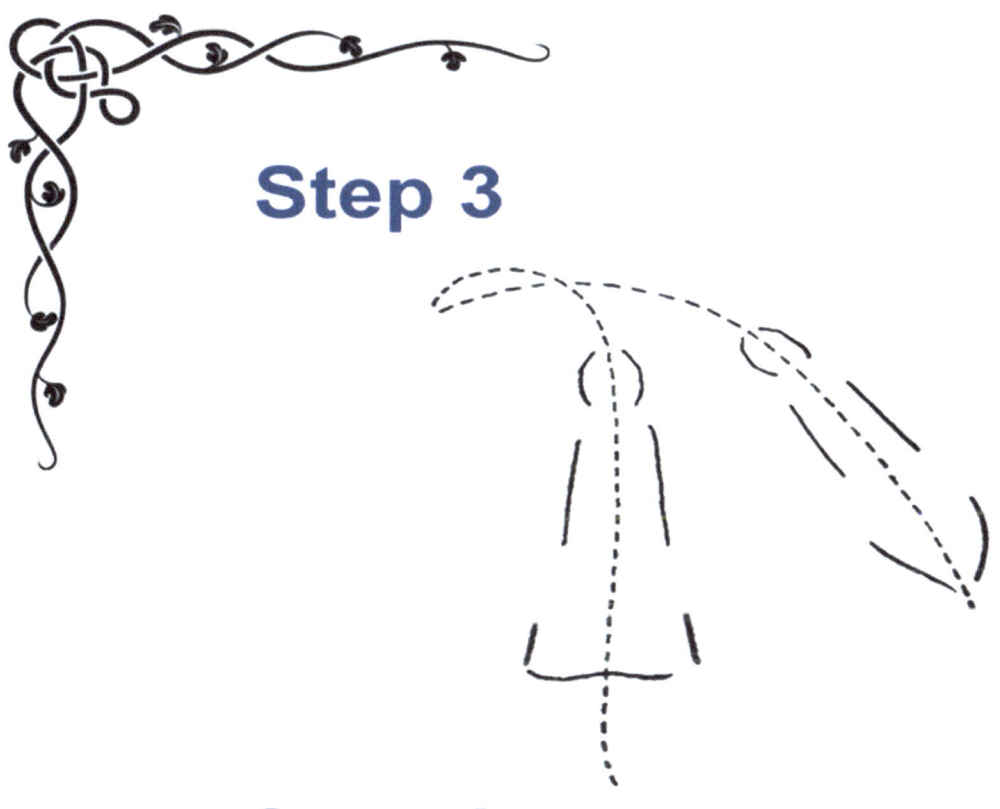

Step 4

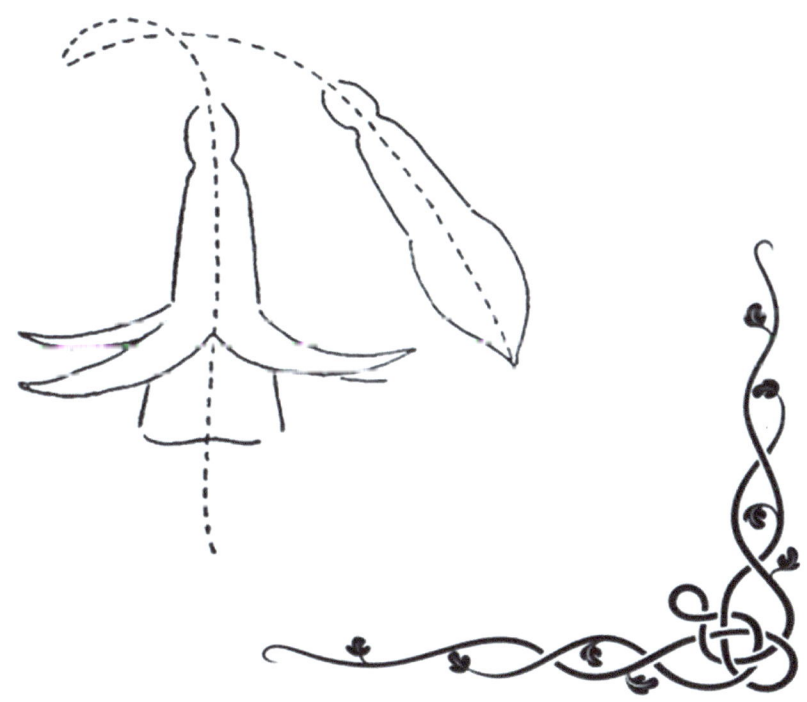

How To Draw Peace Plant

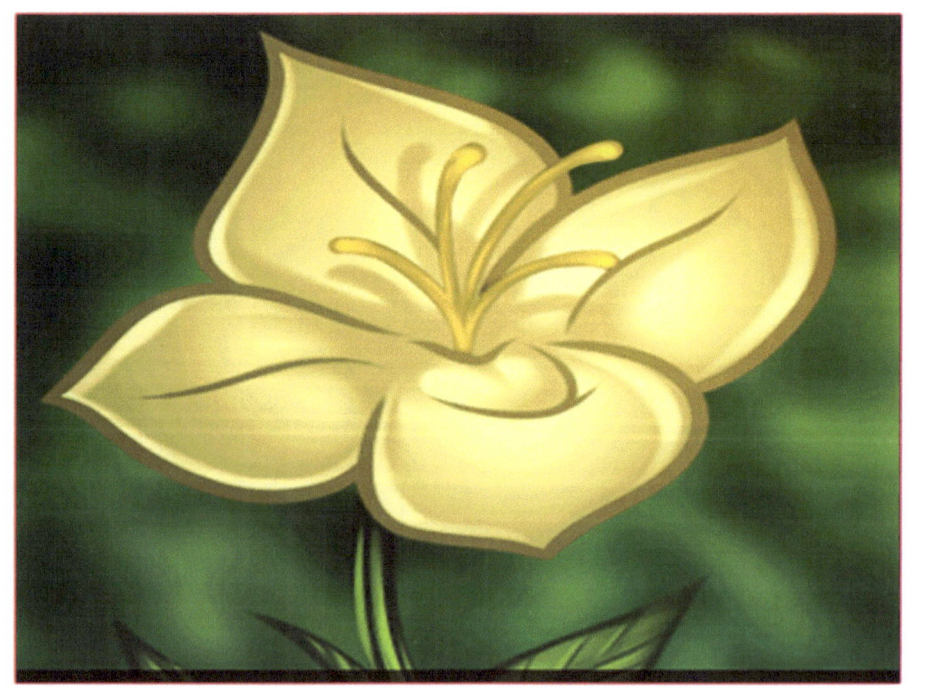

Step 1

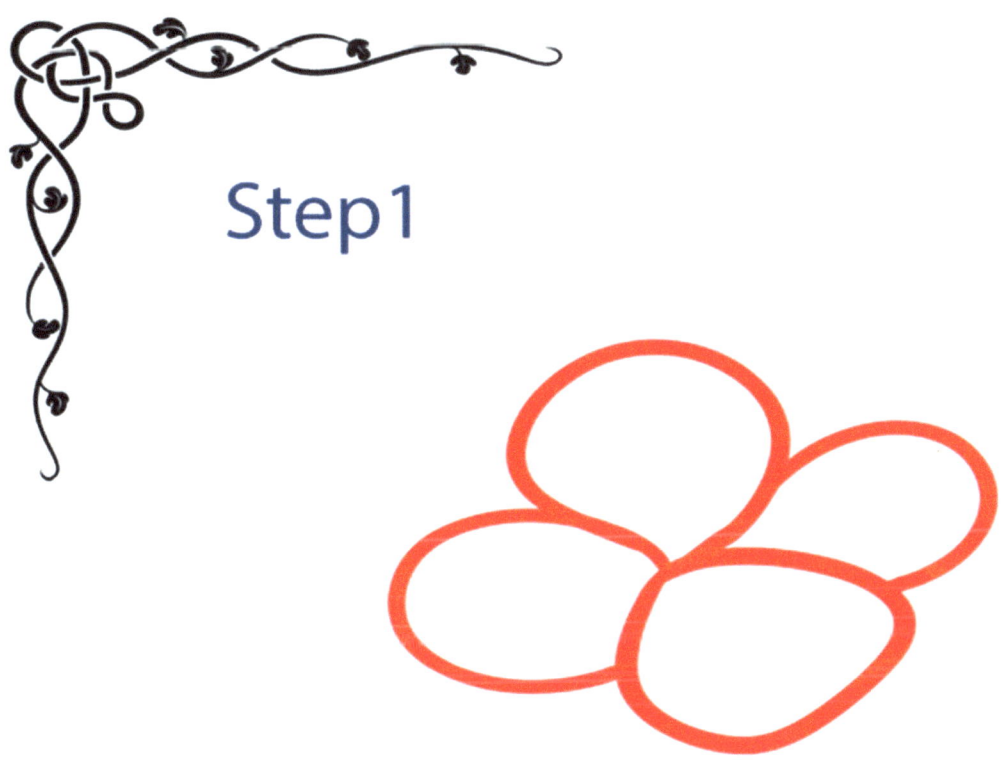

Step 2

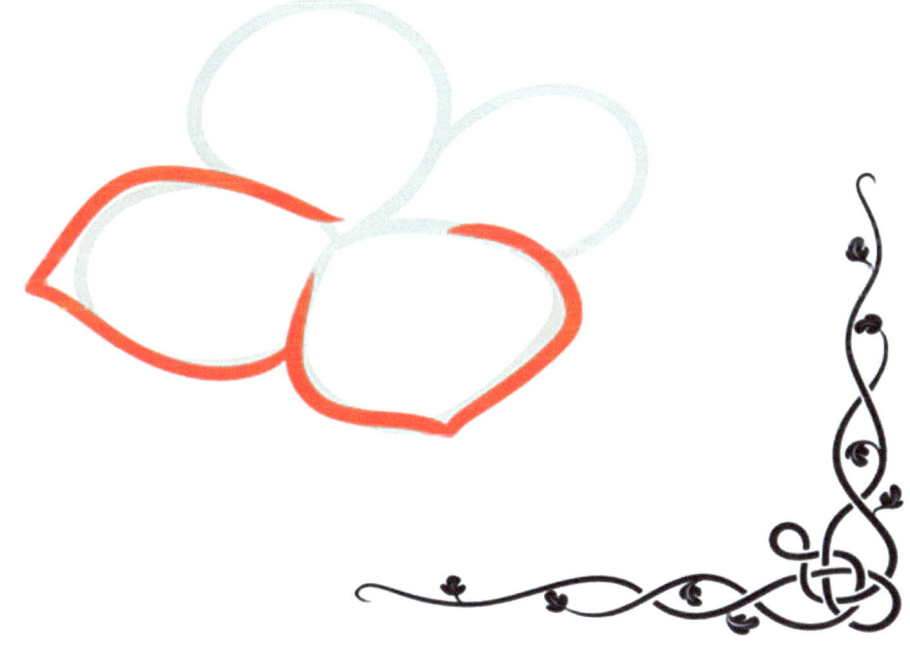

Step 3

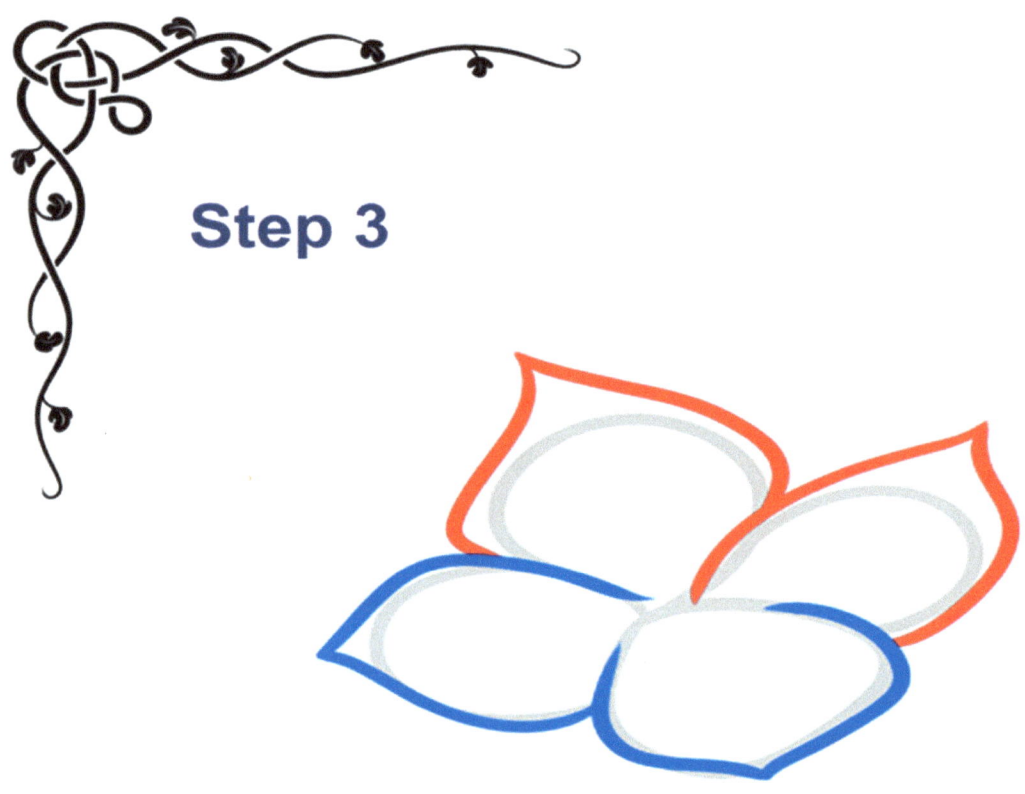

Step 4

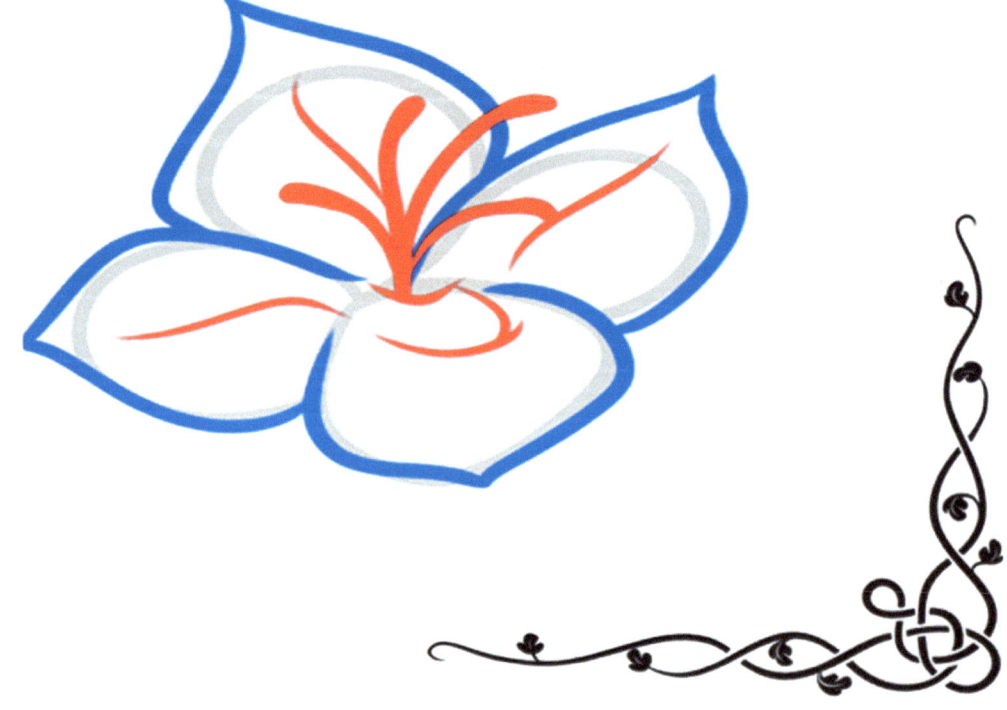

Step 5

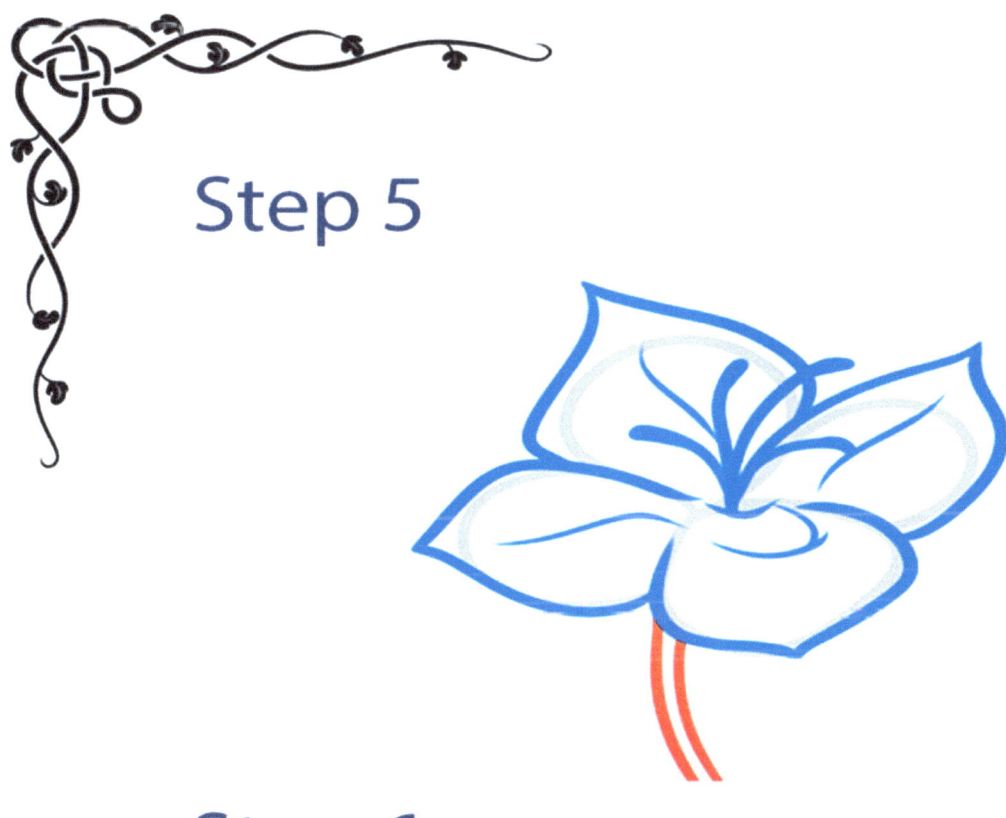

Step 6

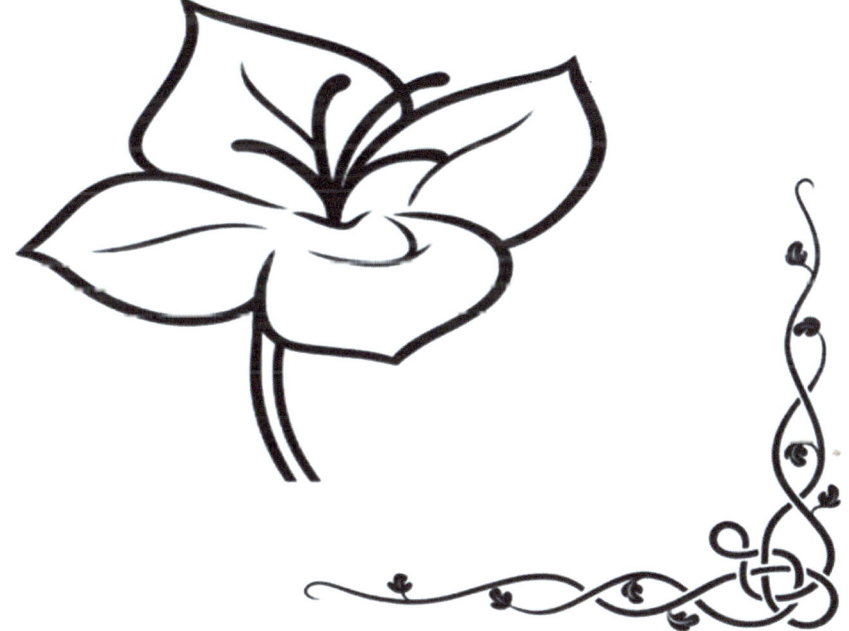

How To Draw
Peace Plant

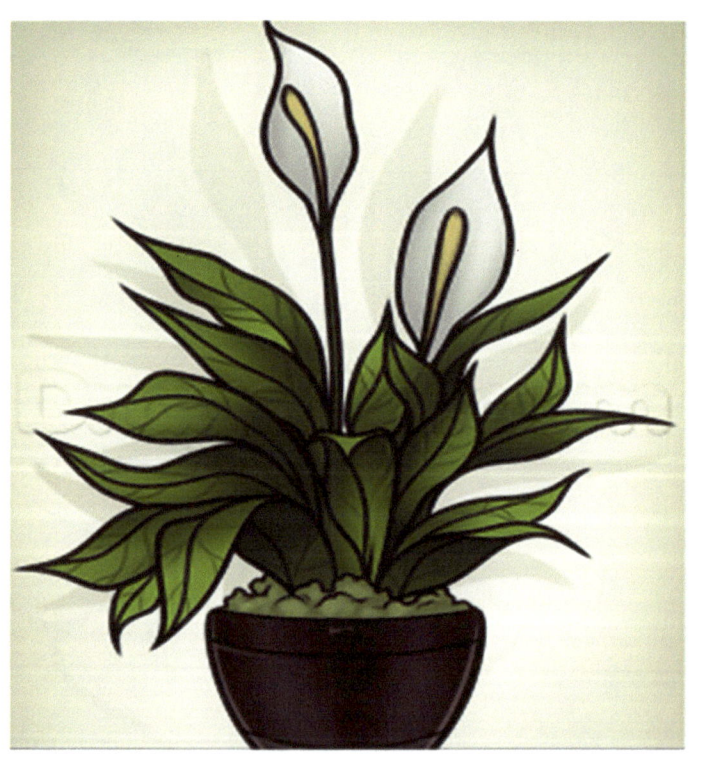

Step 1

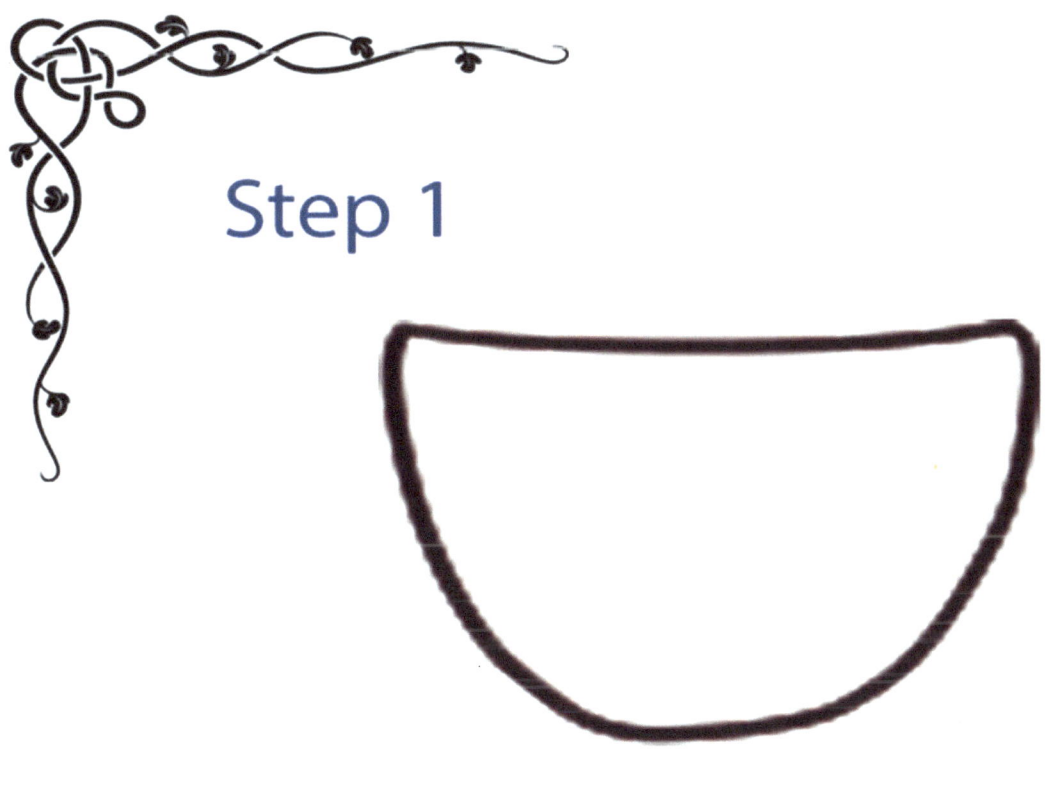

Step 2

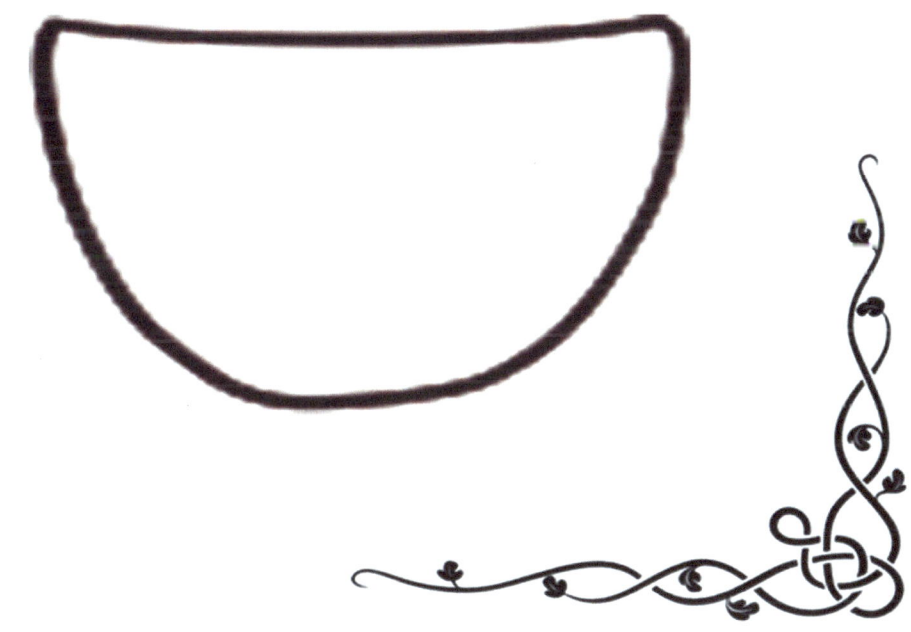

Step 3

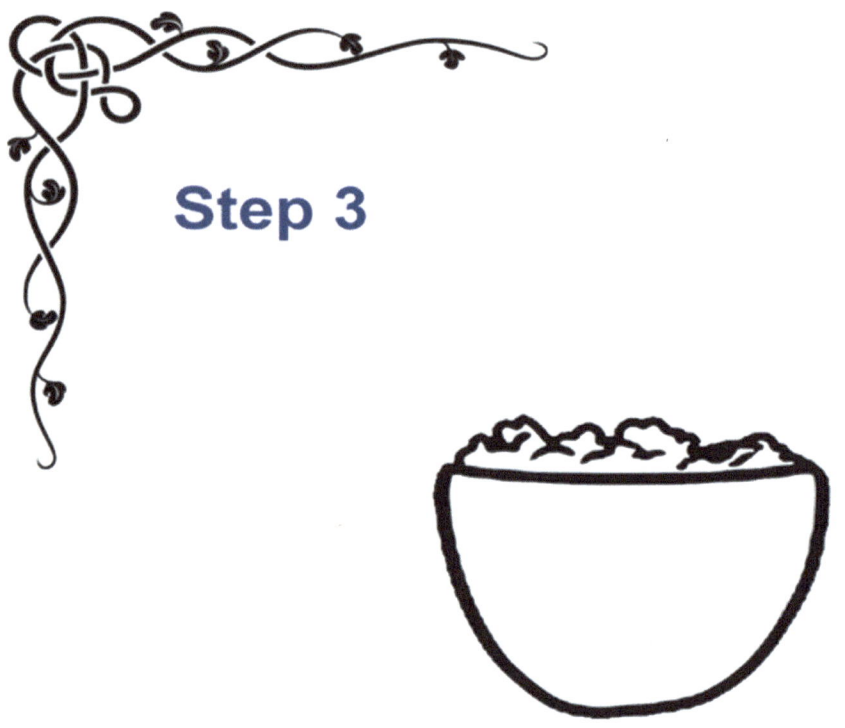

Step 4

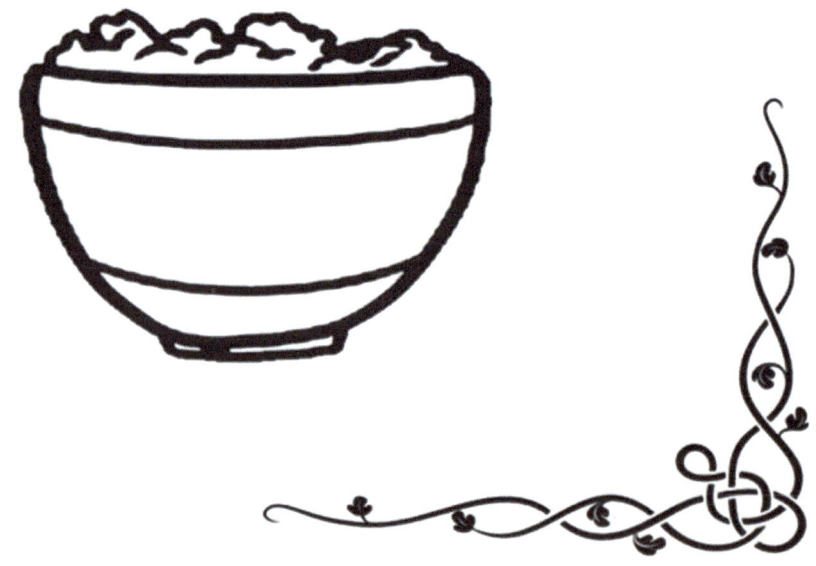

Step 5

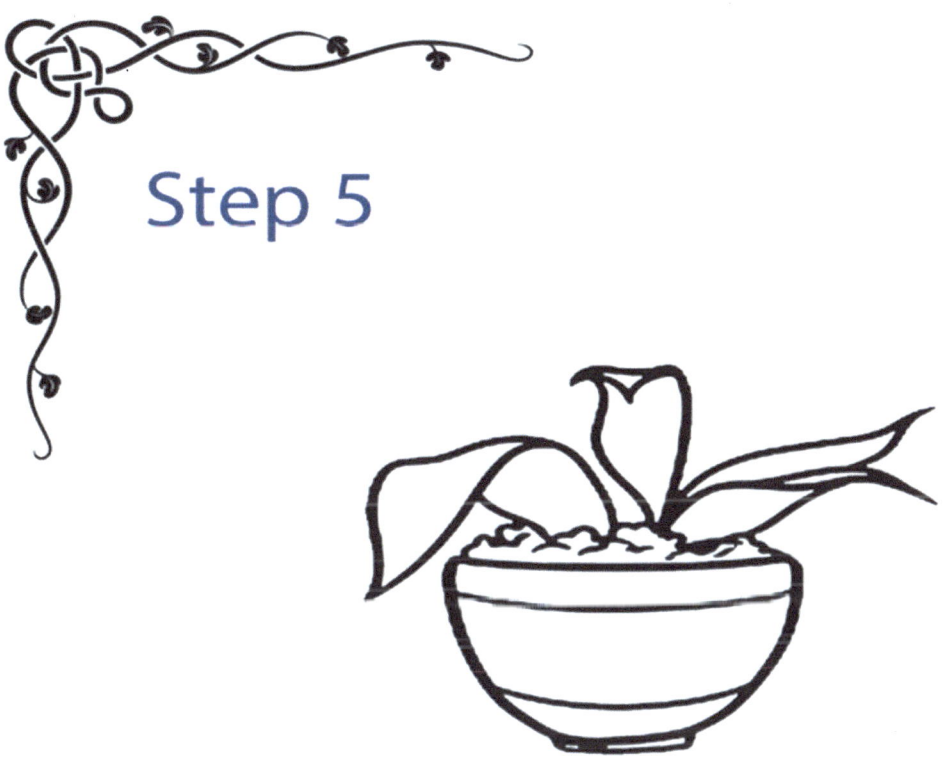

Step 6

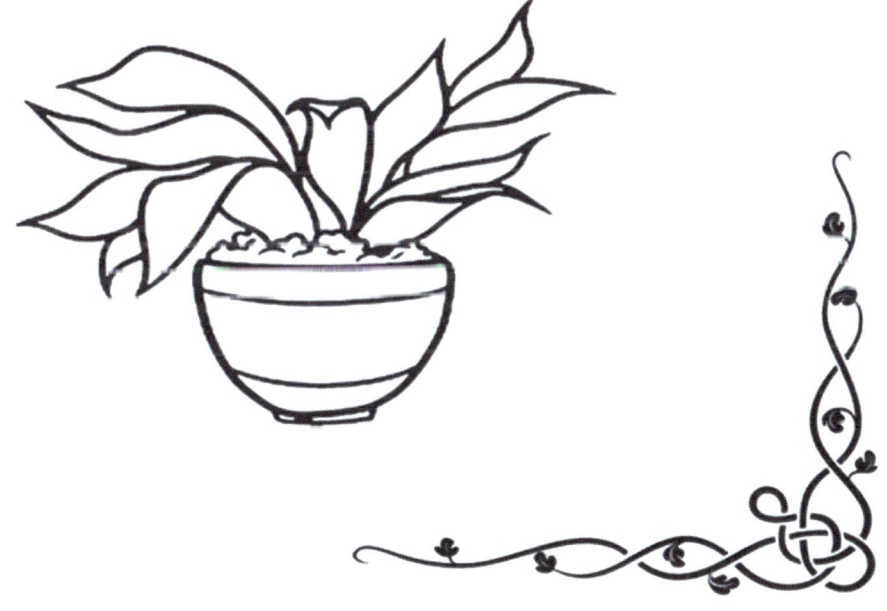

Step 7

Step 8

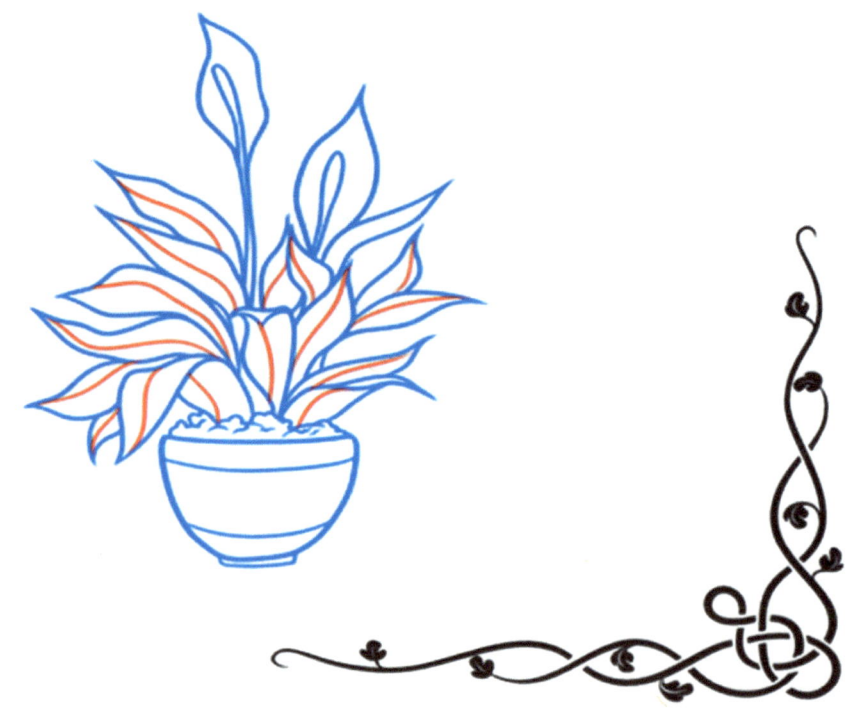

How To Draw
Pansies

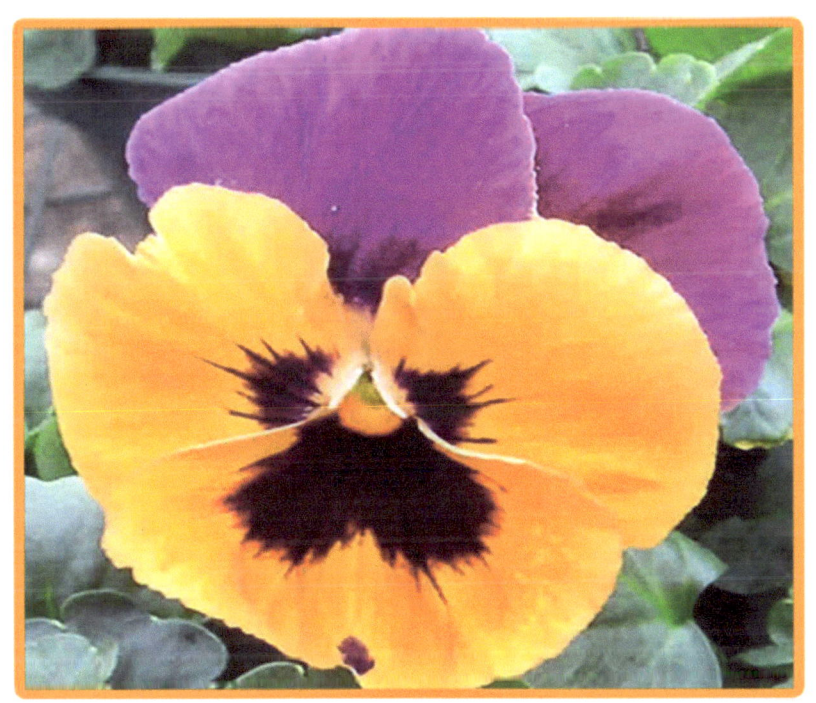

Step 1

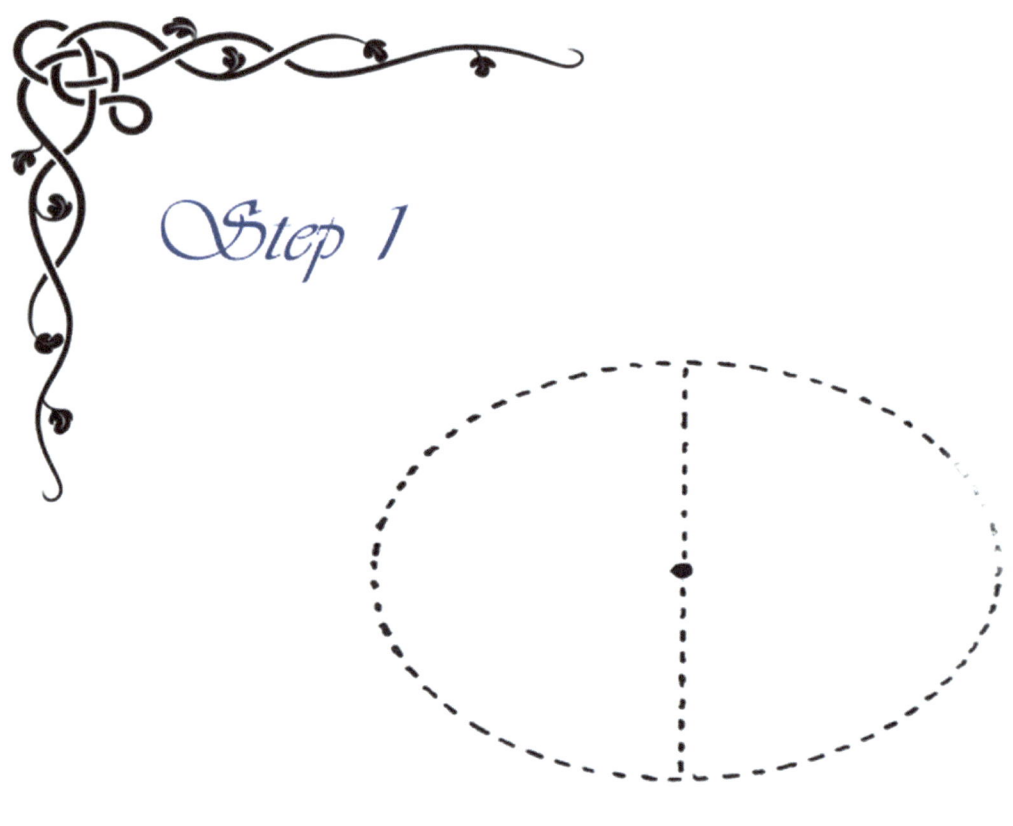

Step 2

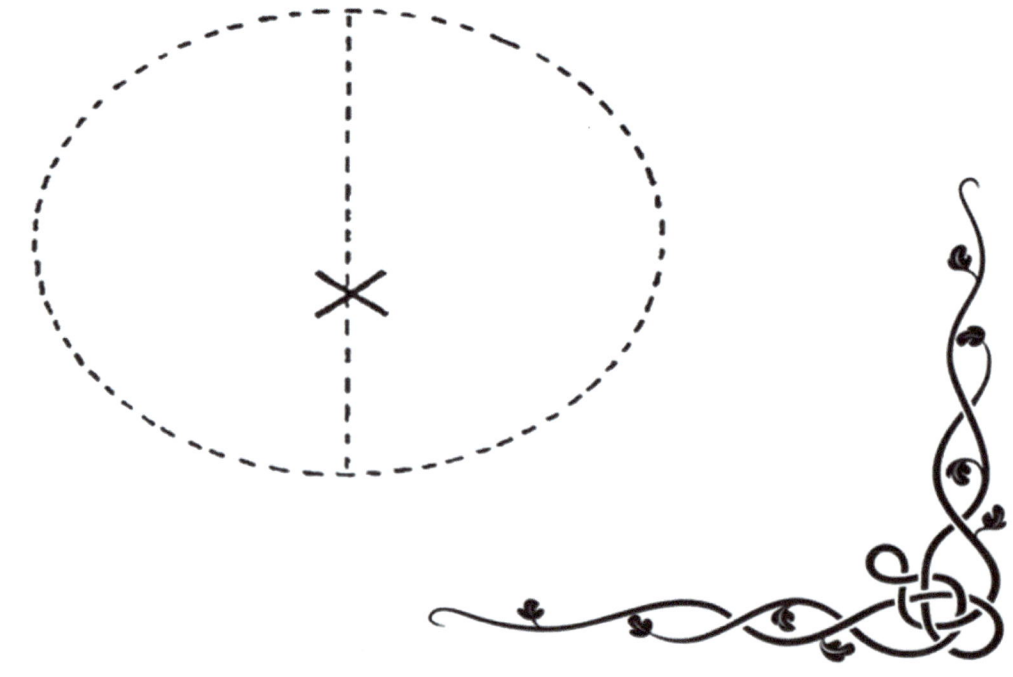

Step 3

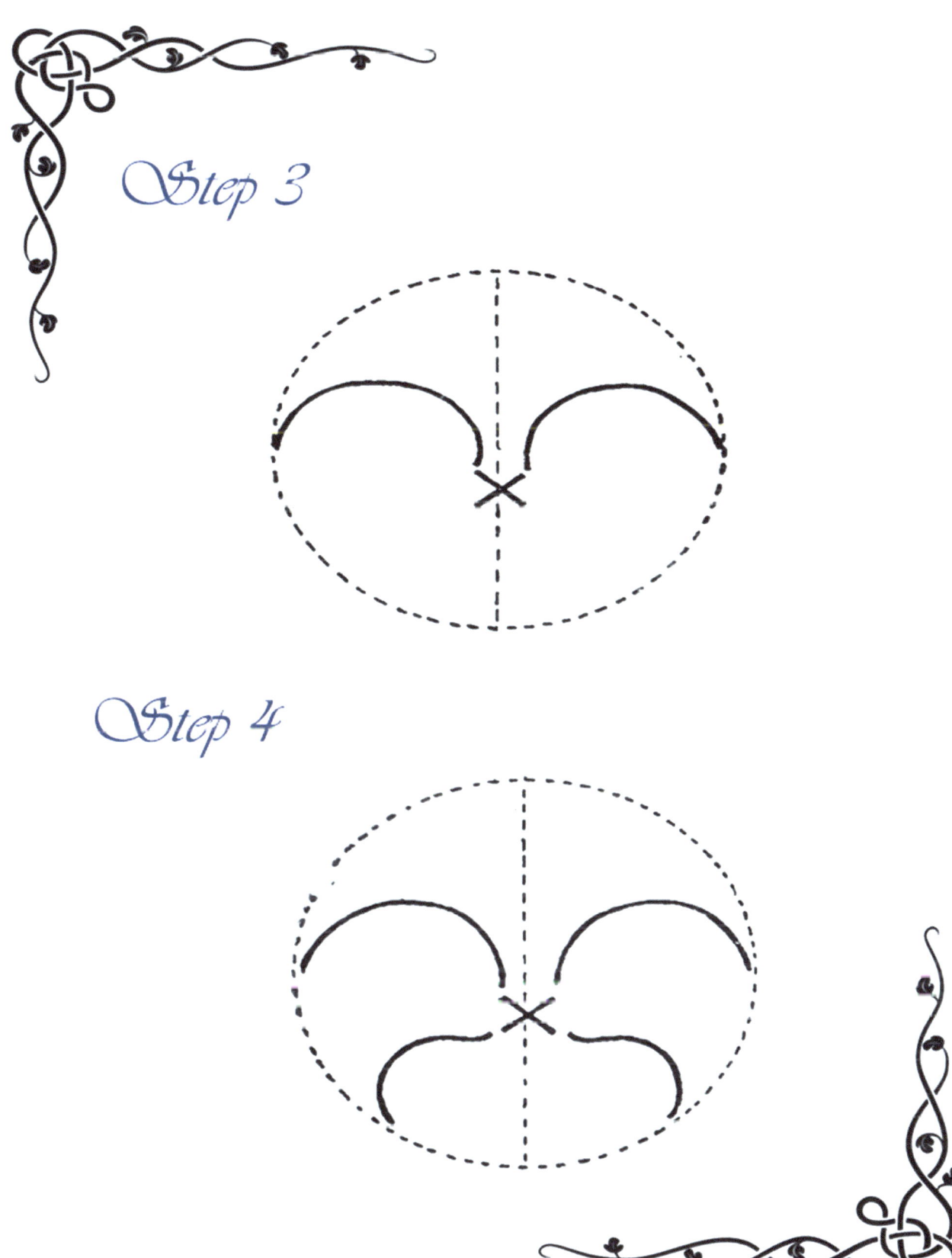

Step 4

Step 5

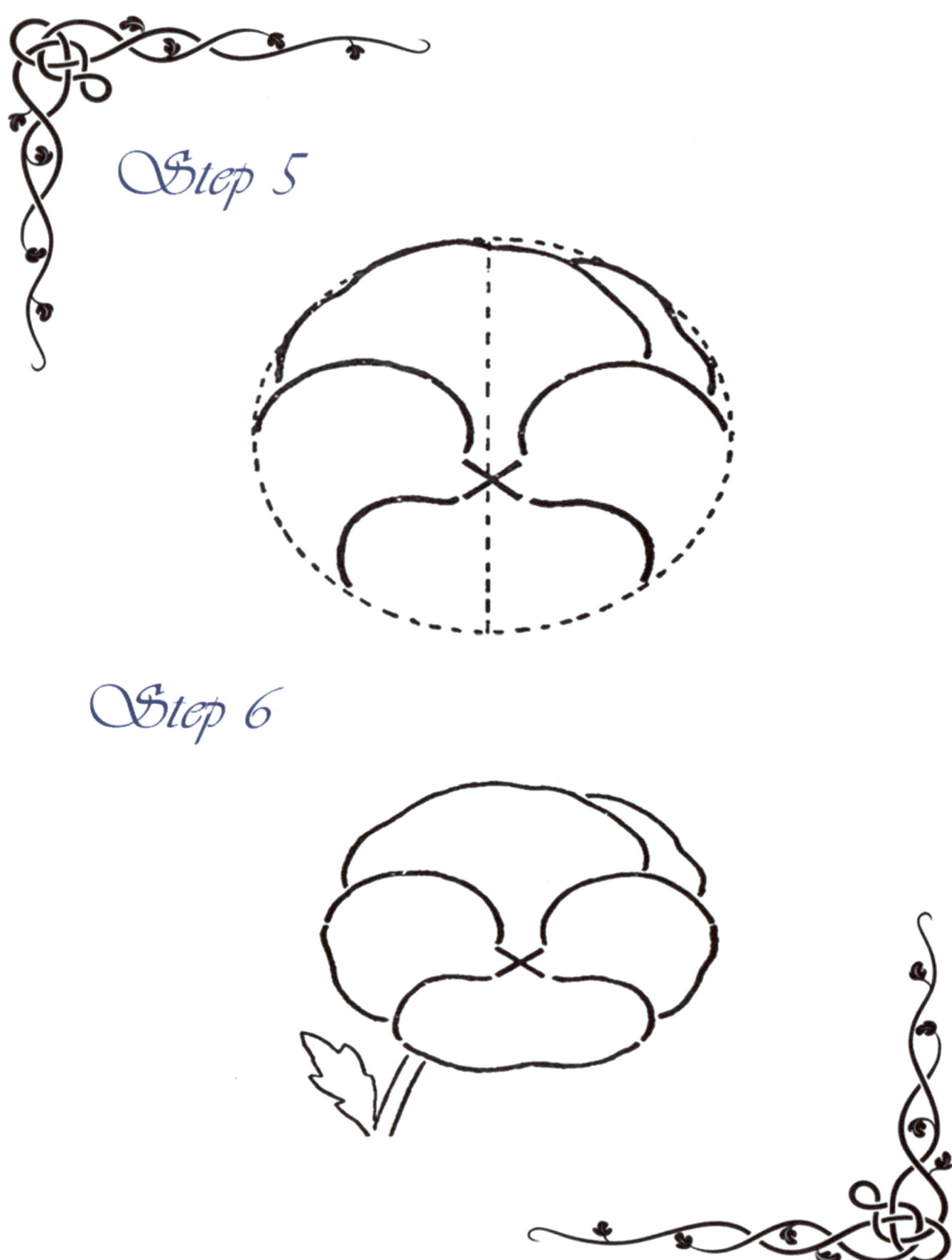

Step 6

Step 5

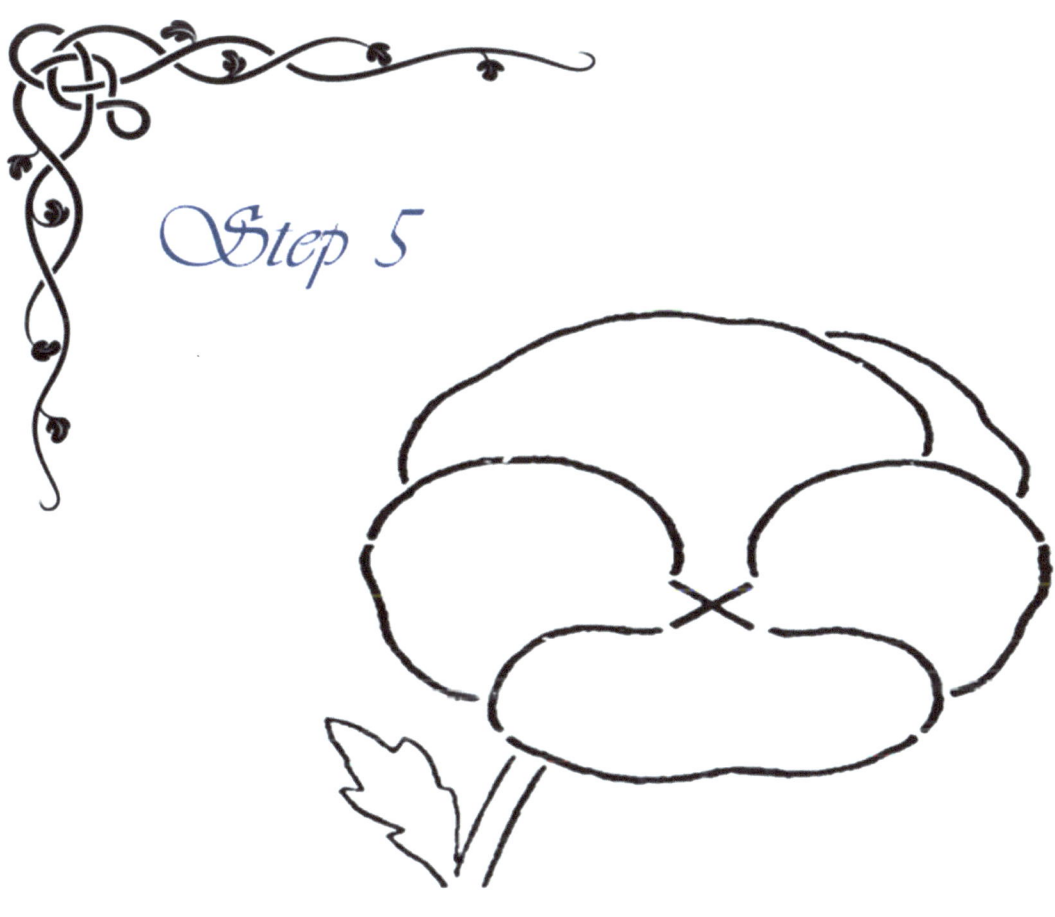

Step 6

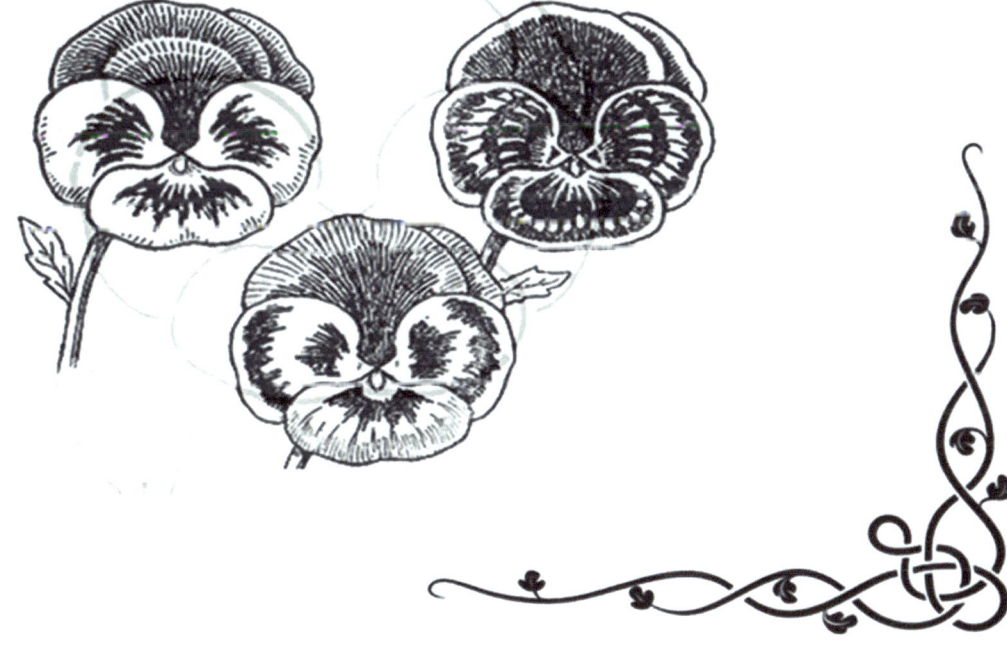

How To Draw
Stephanotis

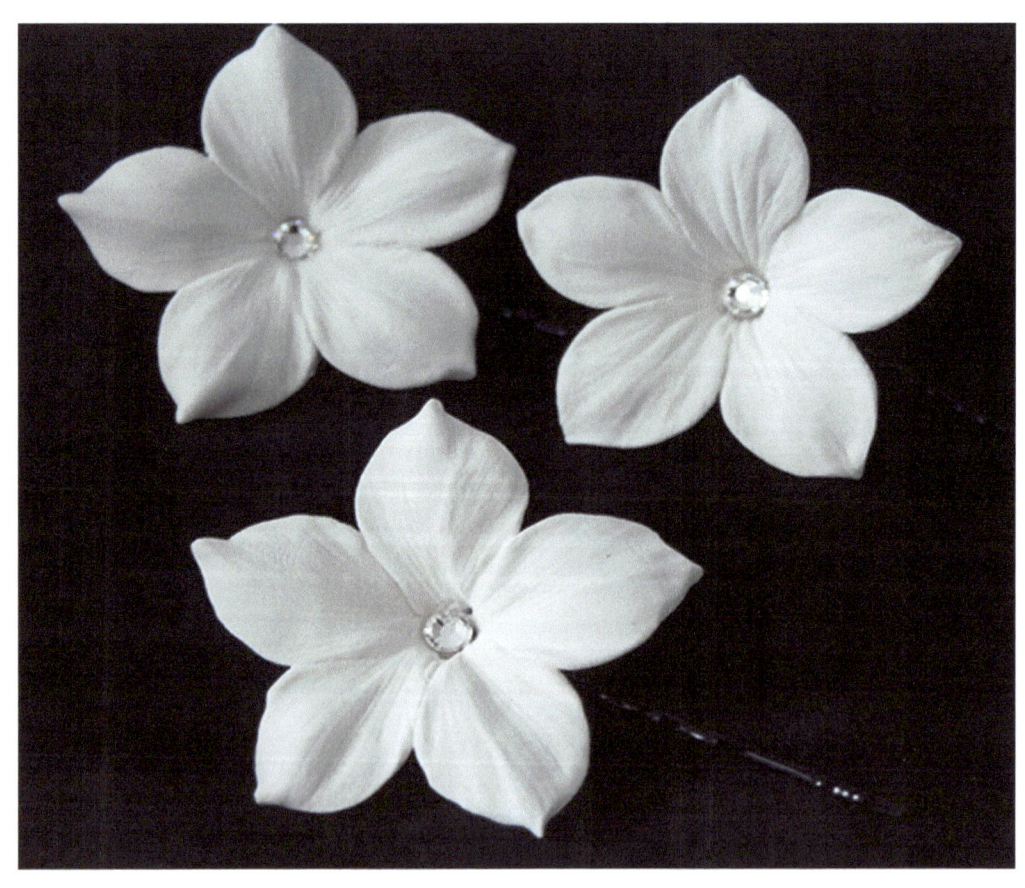

Step 1

Step 2

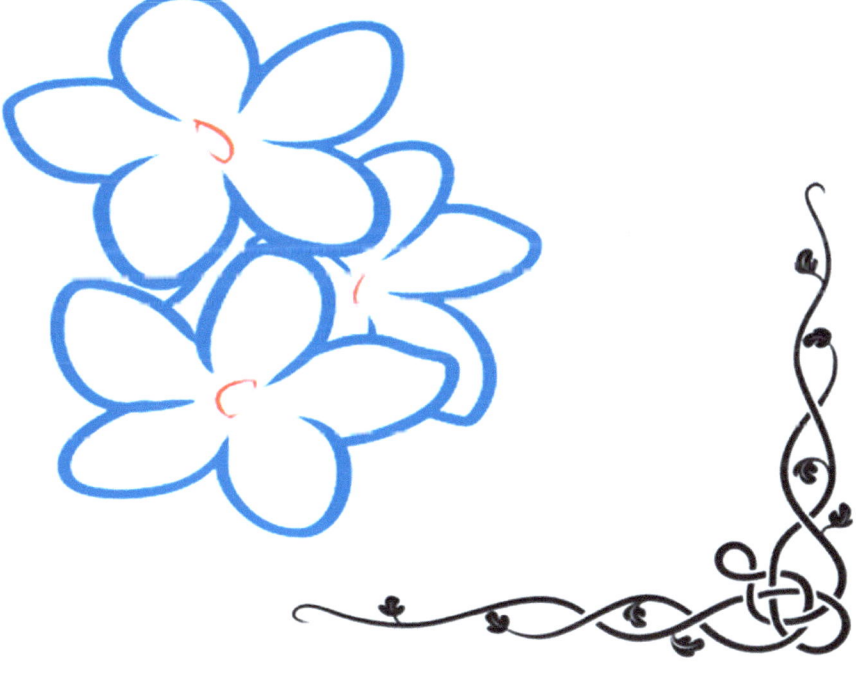

Step 3

Step 4

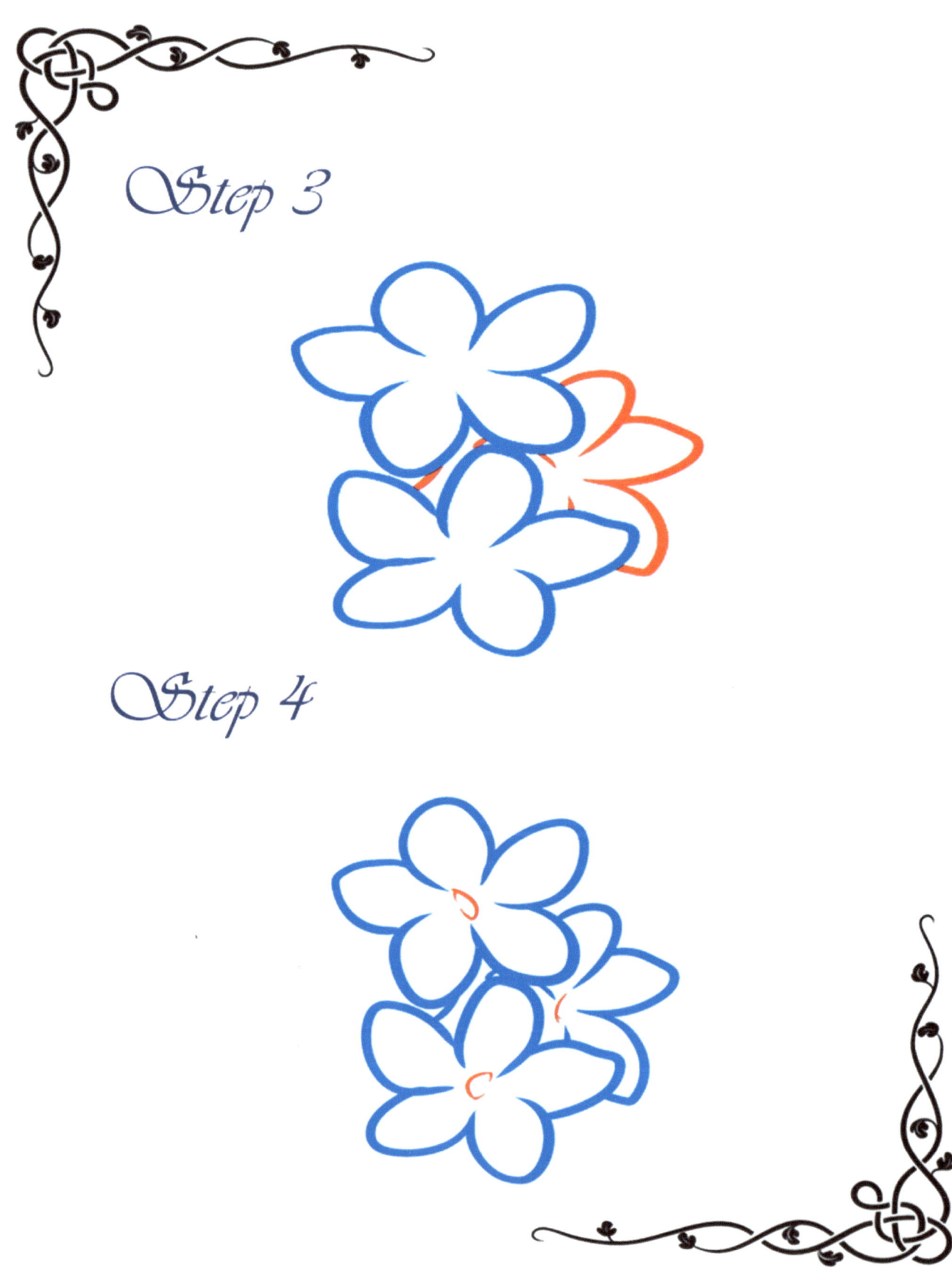

Step 5

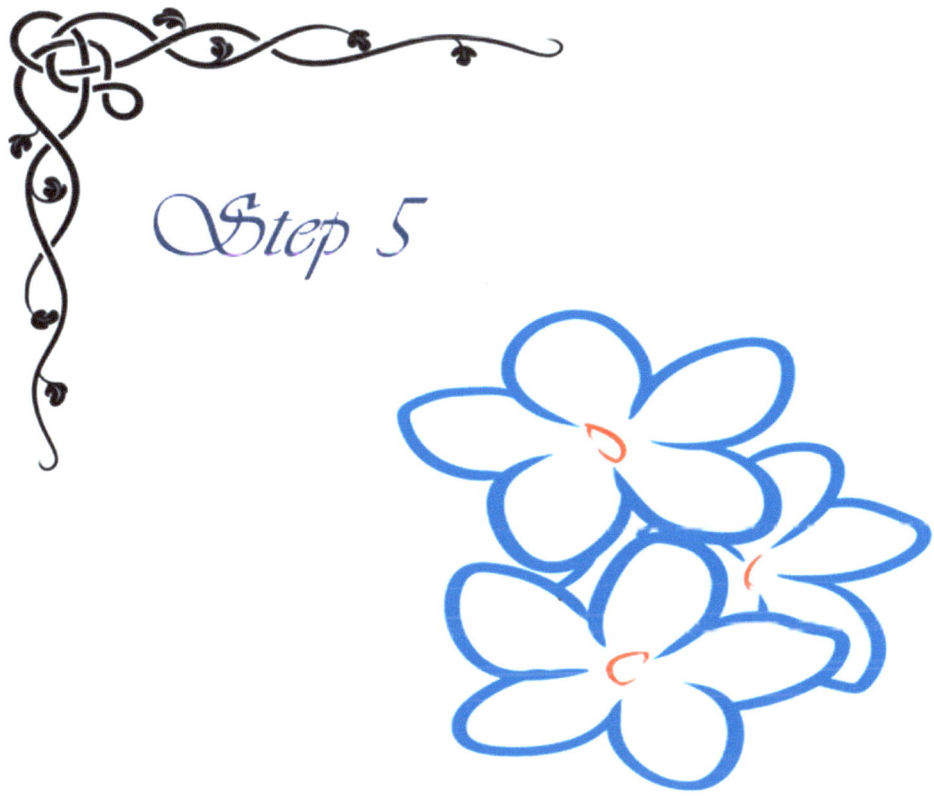

Step 6

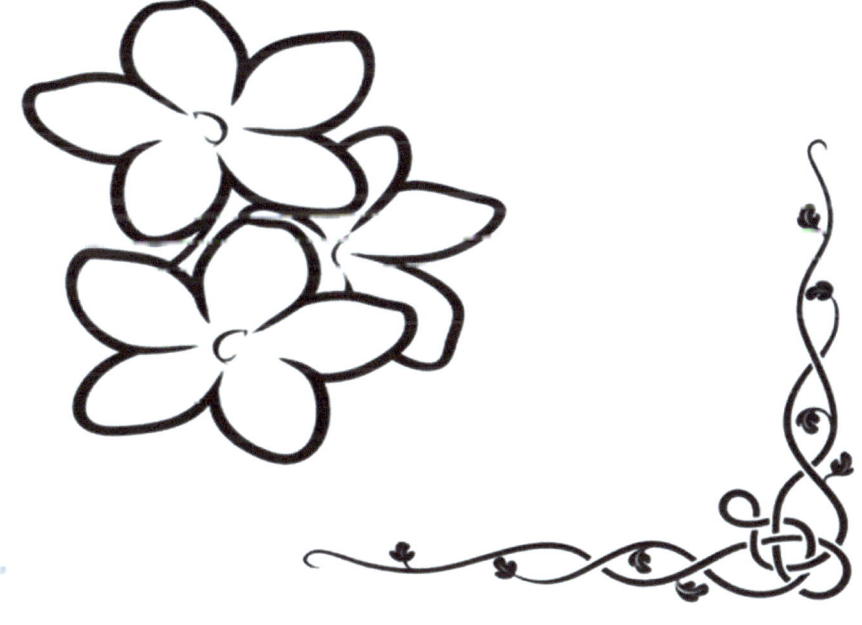

How To Draw Carnations

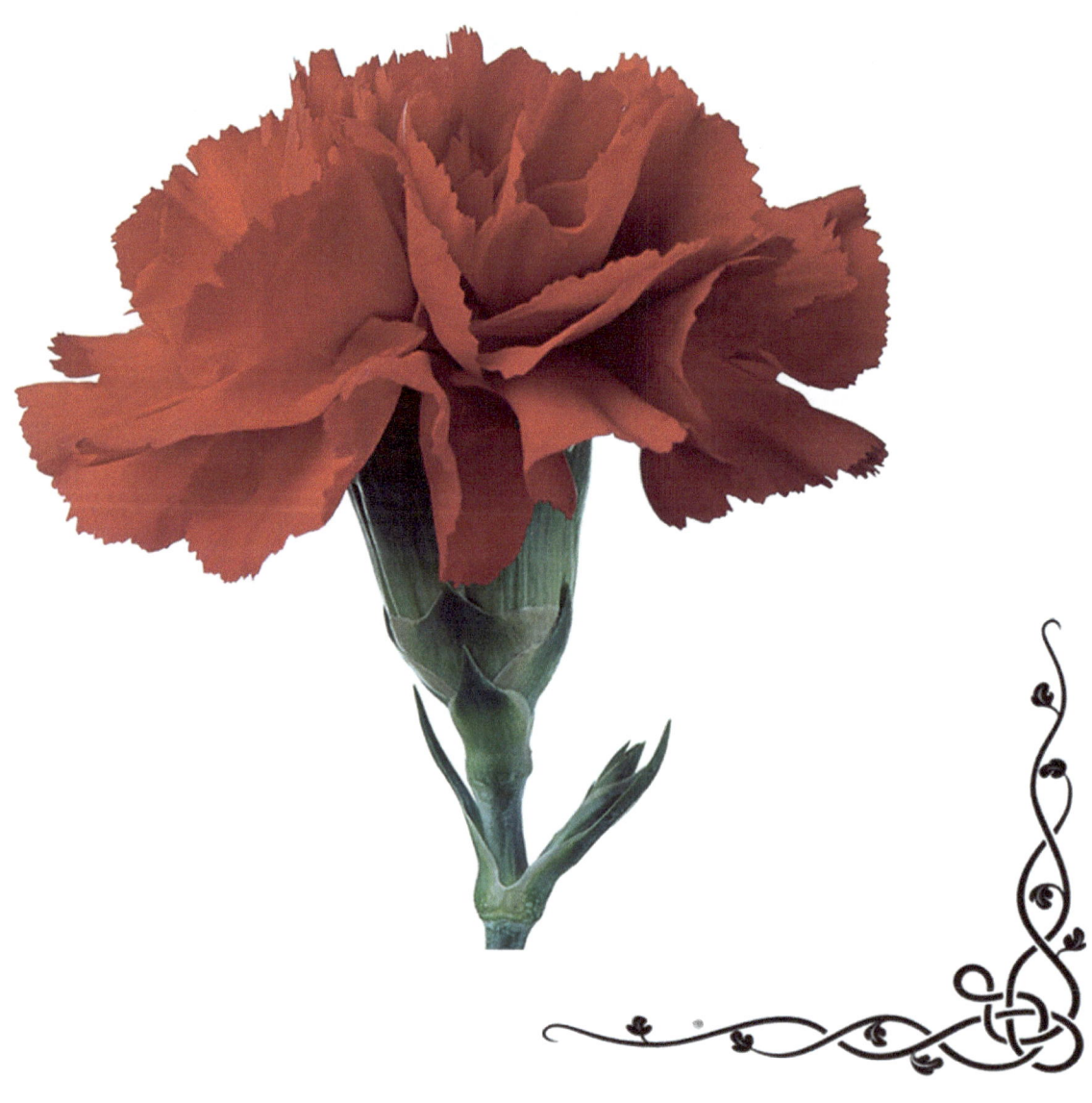

Step 1

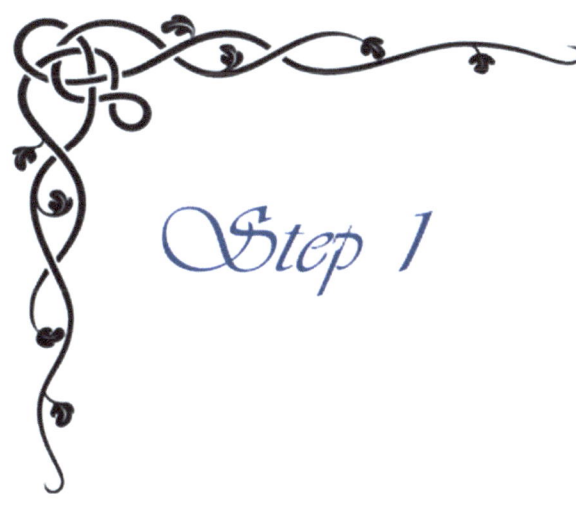

Step 2

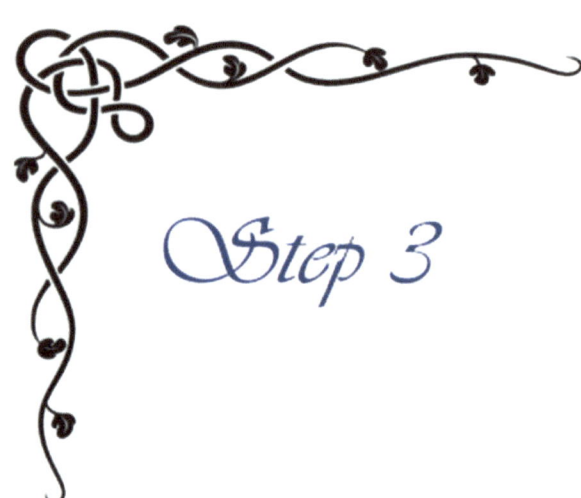

Step 3

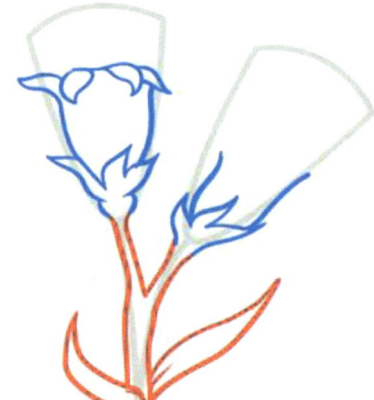

Step 4

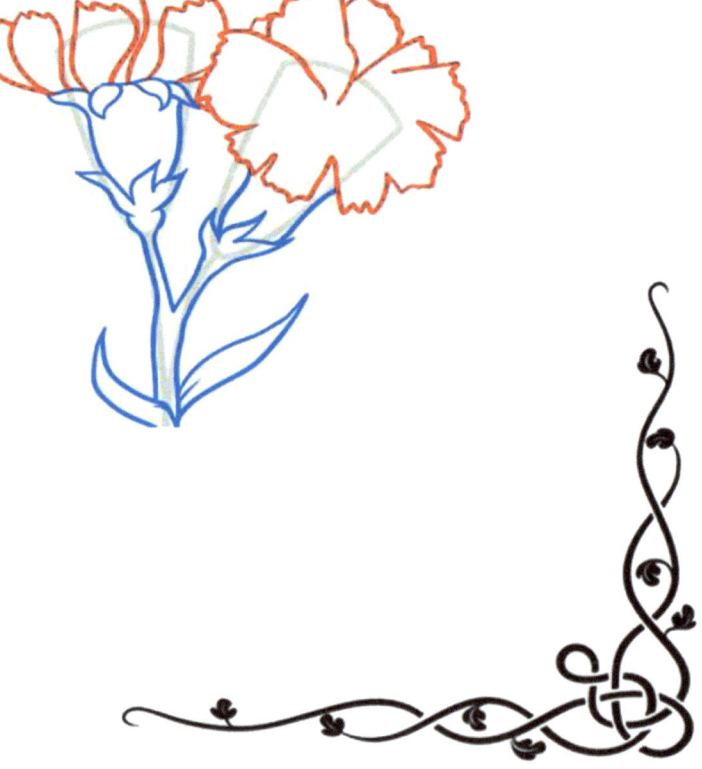

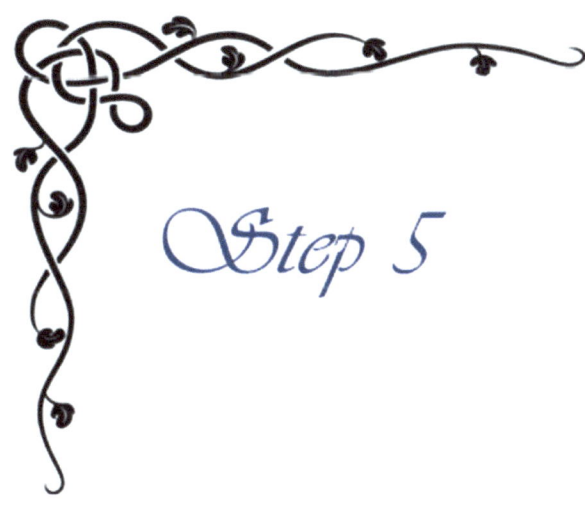

Step 5

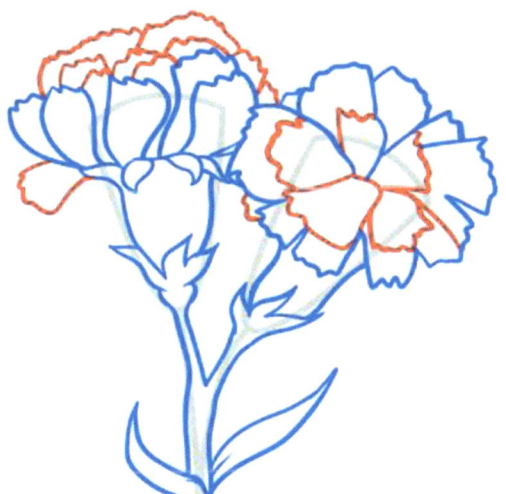

Step 6

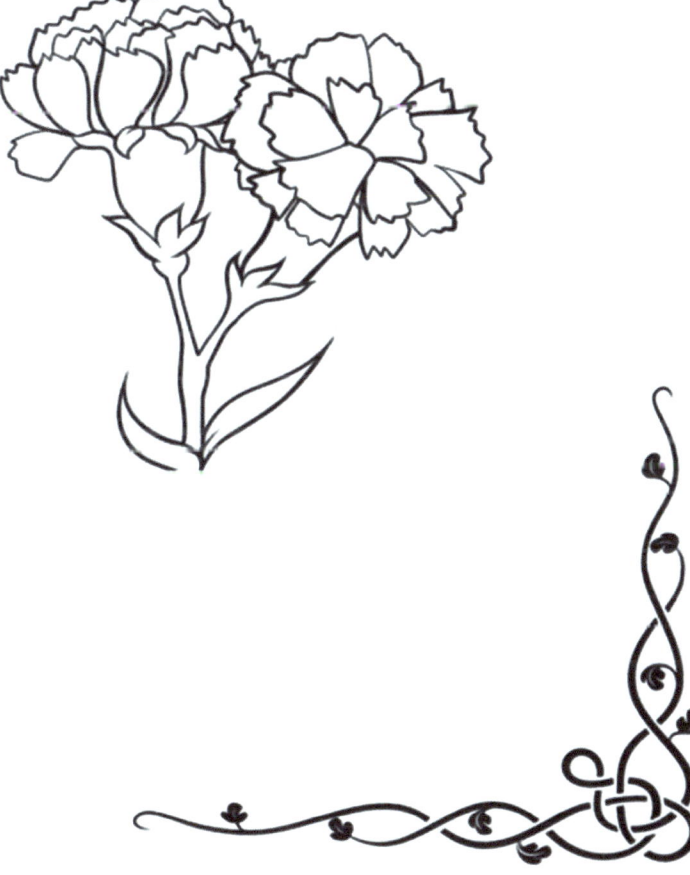

THE END